Building primary care in a changing Europe

The European Observatory on Health Systems and Policies supports and promotes evidence based health policy-making through comprehensive and rigorous analysis of health systems in Europe. It brings together a wide range of policy-makers, academics and practitioners to analyse trends in health reform, drawing on experience from across Europe to illuminate policy issues.

The European Observatory on Health Systems and Policies is a partnership between the World Health Organization Regional Office for Europe, the Governments of Austria, Belgium, Finland, Ireland, Norway, Slovenia, Sweden, the United Kingdom and the Veneto Region of Italy, the European Commission, the World Bank, UNCAM (French National Union of Health Insurance Funds), the London School of Economics and Political Science, and the London School of Hygiene & Tropical Medicine.

Building primary care in a changing Europe

Edited by

Dionne S. Kringos

Wienke G.W. Boerma

Allen Hutchinson

Richard B. Saltman

Keywords

DELIVERY OF HEALTH CARE
HEALTH CARE SYSTEMS
PRIMARY CARE
PRIMARY HEALTH CARE
PUBLIC HEALTH

ISBN 978 92 890 50 319

Printed in the United Kingdom

Typeset by Steve Still

Cover design by M2M

Contents

Chapter 4
Diversity of primary care systems analysed 103
Dionne Kringos, Wienke Boerma, Yann Bourgueil, Thomas Cartier,
Toni Dedeu, Toralf Hasvold, Allen Hutchinson, Margus Lember,
Marek Oleszczyk, Danica Rotar Pavlič

Chapter 5
Overview and future challenges for primary care 119
Wienke Boerma, Yann Bourgueil, Thomas Cartier, Toralf Hasvold,
Allen Hutchinson, Dionne Kringos, Madelon Kroneman

Volume 2: Country reports on primary care
*(separately published and available online, see Building primary care
in a changing Europe – Case studies – http://www.euro.who.int/en/about-us/
partners/observatory/publications/studies)*

Preface

This book is a product from the PHAMEU study (Primary Health Care
Activity Monitor for Europe) that was carried out from 2007 until 2010.
The study has been developed and coordinated by NIVEL, the Netherlands
Institute for Health Services Research, in collaboration with other institutes
in European countries. The following members of this partnership have
contributed to this book. Their names and affiliations are listed below.

- NIVEL, the Netherlands Institute for Health Services Research, Utrecht,
  the Netherlands: Dionne Sofia Kringos and Wienke Boerma
- University of Tartu, Estonia: Margus Lember
- IRDES, Institute for Research and Information in Health Economics,
  Paris, France: Yann Bourgueil and Thomas Cartier
- Heinrich Heine University and University Witten/Herdecke, Düsseldorf,
  Germany: Stefan Wilm and Harald Abholz
- Bocconi University CERGAS, Milan, Italy: Paolo Tedeschi
- University of Tromsø, Norway: Toralf Hasvold
- Jagiellonian University Medical College, Krakow, Poland: Adam Windak
  and Marek Oleszczyk
- University of Ljubljana, Slovenia: Danica Rotar Pavlič and Igor Švab
- IDIAP Jordi Gol, Barcelona, Spain: Toni Dedeu and Bonaventura Bolibar
- University of Sheffield, ScHARR & University of Leicester, United
  Kingdom: Allen Hutchinson and Andrew Wilson
- The PHAMEU study was co-funded by the European Commission
  (Directorate General SANCO).

The project was supported by the WHO Regional Office for Europe, the
European Forum for Primary Care, the European Public Health Association,
and the European General Practice Research Network.

Experts in each country who contributed to the data and information on
which this study is based, are kindly acknowledged. Their names have
been listed with each country chapter. Finally, the authors are grateful to
colleagues at NIVEL for their review of a previous version of the manuscript.

List of tables and figures

Figures

Volume 2: Country reports on primary care

Austria

Belgium

Bulgaria

Cyprus

Czech Republic

Denmark

Estonia

Finland

Fig. A8.2 The development in supply of (selection of) primary care professionals per 100 000 inhabitants in the most recent available five-year period

Fig. A8.3 The extent to which organizational arrangements commonly exist in primary care practices or primary care centres

Fig. A8.4 Patient satisfaction with aspects of care provision

Fig. A8.5 Shared practice

Fig. A8.6 Number of hospital admissions per 100 000 population with a primary care sensitive diagnosis in 2008

France

Table A9.1 Development of health care resources and utilization

Table A9.2 GPs' involvement in delivery of various primary care services

Fig. A9.1 How does the average income of mid-career health professionals relate to that of a mid-career GP?

Fig. A9.2 The development in supply of primary care professionals per 100 000 inhabitants

Fig. A9.3 The extent to which organizational arrangements commonly exist in primary care practices or primary care centres

Fig. A9.4 Number of hospital admissions per 100,000 population with a primary care sensitive diagnosis in most recent year

Germany

Table A10.1 Development of health care resources and utilization

Table A10.2 GPs' involvement in delivery of various primary care services

Fig. A10.1 How does the average income of mid-career health professionals relate to that of a mid-career GP?

Fig. A10.2 The development in supply of primary care professionals per 100 000 inhabitants in the most recent available five-year period

Fig. A10.3 The extent to which organizational arrangements commonly exist in primary care practices or primary care centres

Fig. A10.4 Patient satisfaction with aspects of care provision

Fig. A13.1 The development in supply of primary care professionals per 100 000 inhabitants in the most recent available five-year period

Fig. A13.2 The extent to which organizational arrangements commonly exist in primary care practices or primary care centres

Fig. A13.3 Shared practice

Fig. A13.4 Number of hospital admissions per 100 000 population with a primary care sensitive diagnosis in most recent year

Ireland

Table A14.1 Development of health care resources and utilization

Table A10.2 GPs' involvement in delivery of various primary care services

Fig. A14.1 How does the average income of mid-career health professionals relate to that of a mid-career GP?

Fig. A14.2 The development in supply of primary care professionals per 100 000 inhabitants in the most recent available five-year period

Fig. A14.3 The extent to which organizational arrangements commonly exist in primary care practices or primary care centres

Fig. A14.4 Patient satisfaction with aspects of care provision

Fig. A14.5 Shared practice

Italy

Table A15.1 Development of health care resources and utilization

Table A15.2 GPs' involvement in delivery of various primary care services

Fig. A15.1 How does the average income of mid-career health professionals relate to that of a mid-career GP?

Fig. A15.2 The development in supply of primary care professionals per 100 000 inhabitants in the most recent available five-year period

Fig. A15.3 The extent to which organizational arrangements commonly exist in primary care practices or primary care centres

Fig. A15.4 Number of hospital admissions per 100 000 population with a primary care sensitive diagnosis in most recent year

Latvia

Lithuania

Luxembourg

Poland

Portugal

Romania

Slovakia

Slovenia

Fig. A26.3 The extent to which organizational arrangements commonly exist in primary care practices or primary care centres

Fig. A26.4 Patient satisfaction with aspects of care provision

Fig. A26.5 Shared practice

Spain

Table A27.1 Development of health care resources and utilization

Table A27.2 GPs' involvement in delivery of various primary care services

Fig. A27.1 How does the average income of mid-career health professionals relate to that of a mid-career GP?

Fig. A27.2 The development in supply of primary care professionals per 100 000 inhabitants in the most recent available five-year period

Fig. A27.3 The extent to which organizational arrangements commonly exist in primary care practices or primary care centres

Fig. A27.4 Patient satisfaction with aspects of care provision

Fig. A27.5 Shared practice

Fig. A27.6 Number of hospital admissions per 100 000 population with a primary care sensitive diagnosis in most recent year

Sweden

Table A28.1 Development of health care resources and utilization

Table A28.2 GPs' involvement in delivery of various primary care services

Fig. A28.1 How does the average income of mid-career health professionals relate to that of a mid-career GP?

Fig. A28.2 The development in supply of primary care professionals per 100 000 inhabitants in the most recent available five-year period

Switzerland

Turkey

United Kingdom

Chapter 1
Introduction

Wienke Boerma and Dionne Kringos

Primary care in Europe is facing high expectations. It is expected that primary care can help health systems become more responsive to changing health needs; offer more integrated care delivery; and increase the efficiency of the system overall. Decision-makers are searching for models to redesign primary care systems in line with these promises. At present, however, international comparative information on the structure, process and outcomes of primary care in Europe is limited. This book seeks to meet the need for information by mapping primary care in 31 European countries using a monitoring instrument developed in the PHAMEU project. In addition to describing essential features of primary care, this volume aims to contribute to answering the question of the added value of strong primary care for the performance of health care systems.

1.1 Health care systems facing a diversity of challenges

Health sector reforms in many European countries have been driven by common challenges related to financial constraints, changing health threats and morbidity, workforce developments and growing possibilities of technology. These developments, which have diverse influences both on the demand side and the supply side, prompt health care systems to adaptations and improving responsiveness to current health needs of the populations. The question is, to what extent and under what conditions will primary care systems in Europe be able to contribute to the solution of these challenges.

Although ***financial constraints*** are a recurring issue in health care systems, the effects of the financial and economic crisis since 2008 have been far-reaching. The economic downturn may have created opportunities in health care systems, such as implementing painful efficiency measures or increasing taxation on tobacco and alcohol, but the negative consequences of reductions in public spending on health care are more prominent. In many countries frozen or cut health budgets especially affected the hospital sector and pharmaceutical care; sometimes salaries of health care workers were reduced. As the crisis unfolded, in several countries changes were also made in the scope or breadth of health coverage, for instance by creating or expanding user charges for certain services (Karanikolos et al., 2013; Mladovsky et al., 2012). The example of Greece shows how the economic crisis has negatively influenced access to doctors and dentists, although social protection was formally unchanged and access to general practitioners (GPs) free of charge. It was not the affordability of care that changed, however, but rather the long waiting times and the physical obstacles to receiving care (Kentikelenis et al., 2011). Although it is too early to identify long-term effects of the economic crisis on health, some effects have already become clear, in particular in countries that have been severely hit by the crisis, such as Greece, Spain and Portugal. There are indications that mental disorders and suicide have increased and self-reported health is lower. On the other hand, it seems that the economic crisis has also resulted in more healthy behaviours and a reduction of risky behaviours. Deaths from traffic accidents have been falling in many countries (Karanikolos et al., 2013).

Changing demand has often been ascribed to the ageing of the populations in most European countries. Indeed, the effect of ageing on health care demand is important, but it should not be overestimated. People today and in the near future will not just become older than previous generations, they will also reach higher ages in good health. So data on age-related morbidity and demand from the past should not simply be extrapolated. Most important challenges on the demand side are related to the epidemiological transition in Europe and the indirect effects of demographic developments. These are the growing prevalence of noncommunicable diseases and the increase of more complex demand, resulting from higher rates of multi-morbidity. Health care systems, which are traditionally designed to manage acute episodes of one illness, need more integrated provision of services in health facilities as well as in the community (Nolte et al., 2008). In addition to changes in curative care, prevention and health promotion will become more important to increase healthy life years. If primary care maintains a continuing relationship with patients and an orientation towards the community it may be well positioned to provide preventive services and health promotion.

Demand for primary care may also change as a result of the changing role of hospitals. Supported by technological innovation, hospital stays will generally be shorter and more complex care will be provided in the community. Finally, demand for care is likely to change as patients move from relatively passive recipients of care to more active and well-informed care consumers. Further development of patient empowerment will encourage people who have the capacity to take an active part in their own health and disease management

(Monteagudo Peña & Moreno Gil, 2007). Patient empowerment, new electronic resources and the Internet may reduce the information asymmetry between professional and patient.

Changes on the supply side of health care are consequences of policies to enhance the role of primary care as well as developments in the health care workforce. Enhanced primary care requires new skill-mixes and professionals capable of fulfilling new tasks in a coherent structure. Multidisciplinary team practice is a response to the need for new models of care delivery (Buchan & Calman, 2005). Major trends in skill-mix development are the enhancement of the role of nurses and extension of primary care teams, either in shared premises or in networks. New tasks for nurses can be transferred from other health professionals, for instance physicians. Examples of such tasks are monitoring of chronic disease, delivering prescriptions as specified in protocols and medical procedures, such as taking cervical smears. Primary care teams may be extended to include new functions, such as nurse practitioners, or new expertise on community health or prevention. Collaborative networks may include a large variety of teams and health care workers, together providing a broad integrated set of health care services, for instance for patients with chronic conditions.

Offering GPs more possibilities to work in teams may also help to solve another issue on the supply side: shortages. In a number of countries, there are concerns about the availability of sufficient GPs in the forthcoming years, in particular because the workforce is ageing and general practice is not attractive enough to recruit sufficient numbers of medical students. For young GPs who want a working environment that allows a good balance between work and private life, independent single-handed practice may not be a favourable choice. Creating more team-based practices in primary care may help recruit more medical students to become GPs. In France, where there is a tradition of single-handed practice, a national plan has been successful in increasing the number of group practices and multidisciplinary *"maisons de santé"* in primary care (Afrite et al., 2013). The plan has also counteracted threatening shortages in underserved areas.

A seemingly easy remedy for health workforce shortages is to rely on immigration of health care workers. Two types of health care worker flows can be identified in Europe: one within the European Union (EU) from newer to older Member States (for example, from the Czech Republic to Germany or from Romania to France and Italy), and a second one from outside the EU (for example, from India and Pakistan to the United Kingdom and from western Africa or Maghreb to France) (OECD, 2008). Important issues that come along with migration are the formal recognition of foreign education as well as communication problems that may arise from different languages or cultures.

Relying on migration may have profound effects on the health care systems in the "donor countries" and it may be questioned whether it is a structural solution to shortages (WHO Regional Office for Europe, 2013).

Advances in technology create a mix of challenges in health care. Over the past decades computers and information and computer technology (ICT) applications have drastically changed the work and increased the possibilities of health care workers, and they continue to do so. Advanced information technologies will enable medical record systems to create databases for population-based working, which is relevant for prevention and more integrated collaboration with the public health sector. The impact of medical technology has so far been most dominant in hospitals, but it is likely that it will be sweeping in primary care and home care as well. It is not just health care providers who will be users of medical technology; patients too will benefit from new, smaller and smarter technology. As expanding care options will undoubtedly put pressure on health care budgets, decision-makers may need to take measures to avoid uncontrolled increases in expenditures. For primary care the development of specialized tests for use in GP practices will be relevant, such as rapid office-based laboratory tests or near-patient tests. Furthermore, portable pulmonary function testing has the potential to enhance the quality of follow-up and patient adherence to treatment for chronic respiratory diseases. Miniaturization of ultrasound scanners may give real-time imaging assessments, without any risk to patients. Tests that were formerly exclusively hospital based, such as 24-hour electrocardiogram (ECG) monitoring, may allow patients to undertake those exams at home. Enhanced diagnostics and possibilities for follow-up in an ambulatory care setting may further increase the autonomy of primary care. The development of telemedicine may create the opportunity to operate remote technical procedures or clinical collaborative work. Telemedicine can facilitate access to the primary care practice of specialists' advice in real time, which will improve service delivery in rural areas or in a context of scarce human resources.

1.2 What strong primary care is

Primary care is the first level of professional care in Europe, where people present their health problems and where the majority of the population's curative and preventive health needs are satisfied (Starfield, 1992; Allen et al., 2011). Primary care as an organizational concept should be distinguished from "Primary health care", which has a broader and more political connotation. For instance, the latter concept refers to the reduction of exclusion of patients and the promotion of equal access to health resources, along with the role of leadership and dialogue among stakeholders to achieve that goal – it also covers both health care and other sectors, such as social care.

By its nature, primary care can best be provided close to where people are living and without obstacles to access. Primary care is generalist care, focused on the person as a whole, instead of on only one specific organ or health problem. The mix of disciplines that make up the primary care workforce may differ from country to country, but general practice or family practice is often considered to be the core of primary care. Besides GPs/family practitioners, the most common primary care providers in Europe are general internists, general paediatricians, pharmacists, primary care nurses, physiotherapists, podiatrists, home care workers and mental health care professionals (Health Council of the Netherlands, 2004; Kringos et al., 2010b; Starfield, 1994).

Strong primary care is often associated with the gatekeeping position of GPs; however, the strength of primary care is based on more characteristics than this one alone. The essential role of primary care is as the door to the whole health care system, which requires that it should preferably be offered in the community where people are living, without any physical, psychological or financial barriers whatsoever. Furthermore, a generalist and patient-centred approach is essential, and also that the medical history and the living situation of patients are taken into account. If necessary, patients can be referred to a medical specialist or hospital. The GP will guide the patient through the referral process and the health care system. However, the large majority of the health problems and diseases that patients present can be handled within primary care. Therefore, a broad set of treatment services should be available to patients through various primary care providers who are in touch with one other. In addition to – or in combination with – treatment, tailored health education and prevention can be offered. To improve adherence to treatment plans or preventive programmes, continuity of care is also important. Last but not least, wherever the patient is moving through the health care system, an overview needs to be kept and treatments and follow-up need to be coordinated. The more a primary care system matches this profile, the stronger it is.

1.3 Is strong primary care an answer to current challenges?

Although the evidence is not conclusive, it is widely believed that a well-developed system of primary care has beneficial effects on the health care system as a whole. Systems with a strong primary care level appear to be better able to control costs and have better health outcomes (Boerma & Dubois,

2006; Rechel & McKee, 2009; WHO, 2008). Recent evidence shows that strong primary care is associated with better population health, lower rates of unnecessary hospitalizations and relatively lower socioeconomic inequality. However, overall health expenditures were higher in countries with stronger primary care structures (Kringos et al., 2013).

In response to challenges in the health care sector, reform measures in many countries have sought to strengthen primary care. The question is, however, how strong primary care in European countries is and if it will be able to adequately cope with the challenges described above. Concerning strategies to focus more strongly on prevention and health promotion, primary care could potentially play a role if services are better integrated and providers adopt a more preventive attitude. At present, however, the situation of primary care in Europe does not seem well fitted for these new tasks. The focus is still strongly on curative care and integration both within primary care and between primary care, services and schools in the community is still poorly developed in most countries. Furthermore, necessary outreach and anticipatory approaches are not widespread. It may be concluded that primary care systems may have the potential to include systematic prevention and intervention in noncommunicable diseases, but this ambition is far from being realized in current practice in most countries.

Over the past two decades, most fundamental health care reforms have taken place in the countries of central and eastern Europe that previously belonged to the former Soviet bloc. The old Semashko-types of health care system had to be completely redeveloped. In these countries primary care development has been an answer to the challenge of creating more effective and responsive health care systems. A number of countries introduced a primary care system with family doctors in a gatekeeping position, thus bypassing countries in western Europe that have painfully sought to make modest steps towards a stronger position for primary care (Liseckiene et al., 2007; Grielen, Boerma & Groenewegen, 2000; Atun et al., 2006; Boerma et al., 2012; Groenewegen et al., 2013). Twenty years of health care development may not be enough, however, to develop a primary care system which is strong enough to fully cope with the challenges outlined.

In countries that did not experience such a profound societal transition, reforms have been more incremental. In these countries no fundamental changes have been realized in the relative positions of primary care and the secondary and hospital sector. Where, in the early 1990s, primary care had been organized in a small and fragmented way, and where access to hospitals was relatively easy, this situation basically continued to exist (Boerma, Van der Zee & Fleming, 1997; Boerma, Groenewegen & Van der Zee, 1998; Seifert, 2008; Svab et al., 2004). Despite ongoing efforts in several countries to promote the performance of services at the first level, it is questionable whether primary care is sufficiently prepared to offer a substantial response to the current challenges. More detailed and comparable information on primary care systems in Europe can serve to identify priorities for strengthening the primary care system in each country.

1.4 Conceptual framework

Primary care can be conceived as a sub-system of the overall health care system, with a special focus on the facilitation of the access and utilization of coordinated services for the benefit of a population's health. For reasons of measurability this general characterization should be elaborated. Based on the results of a systematic review, primary care has been unravelled into 10 essential ingredients, called dimensions, which have been ordered into three groups: those related to the structure, to the process and to the outcome of care respectively (Kringos et al., 2010b). The structure dimension refers to the basic conditions that enable a good functioning of primary care, consisting of relevant policies and regulations as well as the availability of financial, human and material resources. The process of primary care includes dimensions relevant to the services that are delivered. A core outcome is improved health of the population, but efficiency and equity are also considered as such. An overview of the three groups of dimensions has been provided in Fig. 1.1.

The *structure* group of dimensions includes:

- governance (e.g. governmental vision of primary care; pro-primary care regulations)
- economic conditions (e.g. expenditure on primary care; incentives and remuneration systems)
- workforce development (e.g. position of primary care workers; professional associations).

The dimensions at *process* level include:

- access to services (e.g. geographical distribution; physical access to the facilities)
- continuity of care (e.g. patient–GP relationship; continuity over time)
- coordination of care (e.g. gatekeeping role for GPs; teamwork)
- comprehensiveness of care (e.g. available medical equipment; breadth of service profile).

The dimensions related to *outcomes* include:

- quality of care (e.g. prescribing behaviour; chronic disease management)
- efficiency of care (e.g. practice management)

- equity in health (e.g. differences related to social status or gender).

Fig. 1.1
A system framework for primary care

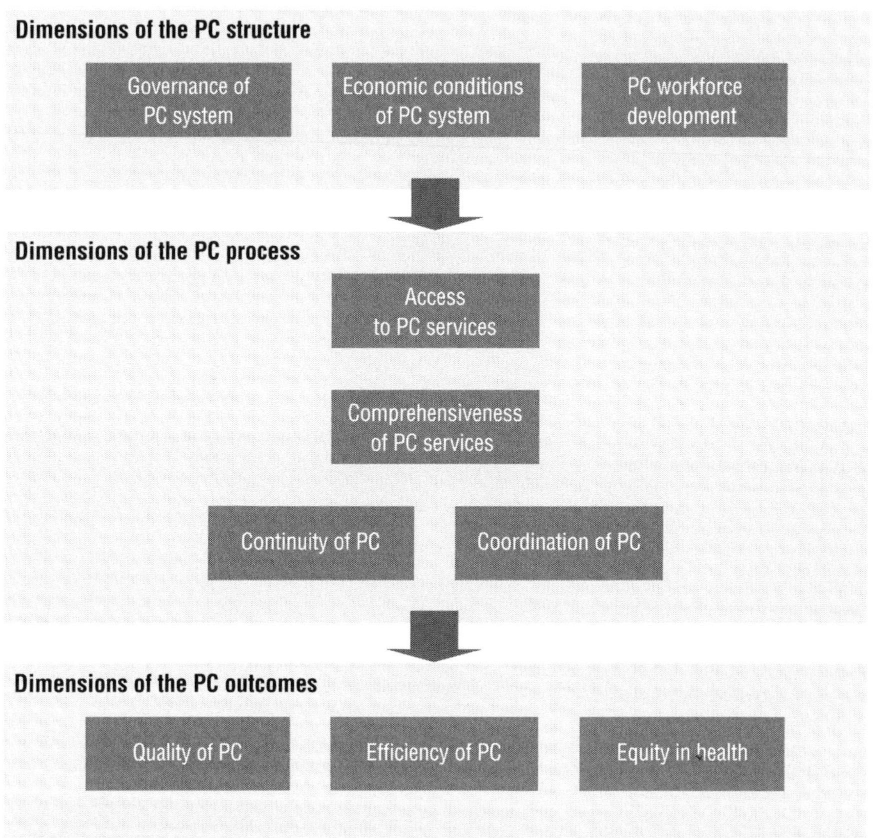

The dimensions identified in the hierarchy of the framework allow a more detailed definition of what strong primary care refers to. In countries with strong primary care a more explicit vision of the elements of the framework has been formulated, including: Do patients experience no or few obstacles to access care, where they are known, at least through a well-kept medical file? Are qualified and well-equipped care providers available to be a patient's advocate and prepared to carry out diagnostics and treatment, if necessary at home? And do patients feel better able to cope with their condition after they have visited a care provider?

As a next step in making the dimensions measurable, an extensive set of indicators was developed for the PHAMEU study. A full list of features of strong primary care included in the study has been presented in Appendix I.

1.5 Methods of the PHAMEU study

The European Primary Care Activity Monitor

A systematic literature review was undertaken to identify the key dimensions of primary care. Each dimension was broken down in to a number of key attributes, which were called "features". To work out the features identified in the systematic literature review, a provisional long list of measurable indicators was made. To this end the selected publications were searched for operationalization of the features. Furthermore, international databases (OECD Health Data, WHO Health for All Database, Eurostat, World Bank HNPStat's, EUPHIX) were searched for "ready-made" indicators. For features where no operationalization was found the research team developed measurable indicators. The long list of indicators was then evaluated on relevance, precision, flexibility and discriminating power, as well as for their suitability for describing and comparing primary care systems across countries in Europe (Kringos et al., 2010a). The final set of indicators included in the European Primary Care Activity Monitor (further referred to as the PC Monitor) is available in Appendix I. Altogether, the nine dimensions have been operationalized into 41 features, 99 indicators and 11 additional information items.

Data collection

On the basis of the set of indicators, data were collected by the PHAMEU project partners in 2009/10 in the 27 EU Member States, as well as in Turkey, Switzerland, Norway and Iceland. Partner institutes in the project were responsible for data collection in their own country and in two or three other countries. The aim was to use the best available data. For some indicators data could be found in international databases, such as from the Organisation for Economic Co-operation and Development (OECD) and WHO. Relevant sources were found via European organizations and networks in primary care, such as the regularly updated "Health Systems in Transition" publications of the European Observatory on Health Systems and Policies, and other international scientific publications. These international sources were complemented by national sources. Where national sources (e.g. literature databases or websites of national statistical offices and important health care stakeholders) could be accessed in a language known by the project team, data was collected by desk research. National experts were consulted to obtain access to grey literature or articles in a language unknown to the members of the project team and to validate the country results. In the absence of written sources, opinions of experts could be used instead. Records were kept from all data sources and from possible deviations of definitions from those used in the study protocol.

On average, countries had data available on 94% of the primary care structure indicators, 93% of the primary care services delivery process indicators and 66% of the outcome indicators. At primary care structure level, there was less data (91%) on economic conditions; at primary care services delivery process level there was less data on continuity of care (87%); and at outcome level there was less data on quality of care (63%). Most countries had alarmingly little data available on quality and efficiency of care. Countries vary much more on data availability on outcome indicators and services delivery process indicators than on structure indicators.

In almost all countries high-quality primary care information on comprehensive aspects was lacking.

Rating the strength of primary care

To determine the strength of primary care, country data on all indicators were transformed into scores indicating the level of primary care orientation of health care systems, ranging from 1 (low primary care orientation) to 3 (high primary care orientation).

The rating of qualitative indicators was derived from the findings of the systematic literature review. For example, if an explicit pro-primary care policy was in place that country received the score "3" for that indicator. Similarly, if GPs were paid a mix of fee-for-service, capitation and performance payment, this was considered as a primary care strengthening incentive structure and so the country received a "3" on the respective indicators. For the scoring of quantitative indicators the direction of scoring (high, medium or low primary care orientation), and the distribution of data among all 31 countries were taken into account. The limits between the scores high (3), medium (2) and low (1) were determined by the 33rd and 67th percentiles of valid country results. So, the scores reflected the relative levels of primary care orientation across Europe. If the indicator of "percentage of total health expenditures spent on primary care" is taken as an example: the lower one-third of countries devoted between 4.7% and 9.8% to primary care, and therefore scored "1". The middle third of the countries had expenditures for primary care between 9.8% and 14.0%, resulting in score "2". The one-third of countries with a higher proportion than 14.0% received the score "3". The score limits have been defined for all indicators in a similar way. A specification of the rationale for the scoring of each indicator as well as the applied score has been provided in Appendix II.

1.6 What this book adds to current knowledge

Almost 20 years ago, the European Study of General Practice Task Profiles produced a Europe-wide comparative overview of the diversity of primary medical care (Boerma, Van der Zee & Fleming, 1997). The study, focusing on general practice only, clarified relationships between health system features and the provision of services. In a study not limited to Europe, Barbara Starfield and colleagues (Macinko, Starfield & Shi, 2003) established a relationship between strong primary care and health outcome measures. The study showed, at an aggregate level, that strength of primary care was related to cost-containment and better health outcomes. However, the role of structures, strategies and characteristics of service delivery that are conducive to strong primary care largely remained to be disclosed. Until now, such information was either completely absent (for instance on all Member States that entered the EU in 2004 and later) or outdated and not easy to compare. This book provides an updated overview of the state of primary care in 31 European countries.

1.7 Structure of this book

In this introductory chapter the challenges of health care systems in Europe have been sketched and the possibilities that well-developed primary care can be a response have been discussed. This chapter also described the definitions, conceptual framework and methods used.

In line with the distinction made in the conceptual framework, chapters 2 and 3 deal with the performance of primary care systems at structure and process level respectively. Chapter 2 shows the diversity of structure and organization in primary care across Europe in a comparative perspective and concludes with a comparison of the governance, financing and workforce development conditions. Chapter 3 addresses the breadth of services delivered in primary care in European countries, as well as variations regarding their accessibility, continuity and coordination; it concludes with a mapping exercise of the achieved comprehensiveness, accessibility, and continuity and coordination of care in countries across Europe, showing also the interrelations across dimensions. Starting from a description of the international diversity of structural aspects and the process of service delivery, chapter 4 focuses on the underlying sources of variation and provides insight into the contribution of primary care to important health care system outcomes.

Chapter 5 provides an overview of the results and their implications, and reflects on the situation of primary care in Europe, including suggested priority areas. Furthermore, options and requirements for future monitoring of primary care in Europe are addressed.

In Volume 2, structured summaries of the state of primary care in 31 countries are presented. These summaries include the following topics: the context of the primary care system; the governance and economic conditions of the system; the development of the primary care workforce; how primary care services are delivered; and the quality and efficiency of the primary care system. Appendix I provides an explanation of the PC Monitor, while Appendix II specifies the scoring of indicators used in the Monitor.

References

Afrite A et al. (2013). *The impact of multi-professional group practices on healthcare supply. Evaluation aims and methods for "maisons", "pôles de santé" and "centres de santé" within the framework of experiments with new mechanisms of remuneration.* Paris, IRDES (Questions d'économie de la santé no. 189).

Allen J et al. (2011). *The European definition of general practice / family medicine.* WONCA (http://www.woncaeurope.org/content/european-definition-general-practice-family-medicine-edition-2011, accessed 18 March 2014).

Atun RA et al. (2006). Introducing a complex health innovation – primary health care reforms in Estonia (multimethods evaluation). *Health Policy,* 79:79–91.

Boerma WGW, Dubois CA (2006). Mapping primary care across Europe. In: Saltman RB, Rico A, Boerma WGW, eds. *Primary care in the driver's seat? Organisational reform in European primary care.* Maidenhead, Open University Press:22–49.

Boerma WGW, Van der Zee J, Fleming DM (1997). Service profiles of general practitioners in Europe. *British Journal of General Practice,* 47:481–486.

Boerma WGW, Groenewegen PP, Van der Zee J (1998). General practice in urban and rural Europe: the range of curative services. *Social Science & Medicine,* 4:445–453.

Boerma WGW et al. (2012). *Evaluation of the organization and provision of primary care in Romania. A survey-based project.* Copenhagen: WHO Regional Office for Europe.

Buchan J, Calman L (2005). *Skill-mix and policy change in the health workforce: nurses in advanced roles.* Paris, OECD (OECD Health Working Papers, No. 17).

Grielen SJ, Boerma WGW, Groenewegen PPG (2000). Unity or diversity? Task profiles of general practitioners in Central and Eastern Europe. *European Journal of Public Health,* 10(4):249–254.

Groenewegen PP et al. (2013). Strengthening weak primary care systems: steps towards stronger primary care in selected western and eastern European countries. *Health Policy*, 113(1):170–179.

Health Council of the Netherlands (2004). *European primary care*. The Hague, Health Council of the Netherlands.

Karanikolos M et al. (2013). Health in Europe 7: Financial crisis, austerity, and health in Europe. *The Lancet*, 381(9874):1323–1331.

Kentikelenis A et al. (2011). Health effects of an economic crisis: omens of a Greek tragedy. *The Lancet*, 378:1457–1458.

Kringos DS et al. (2010a). The European Primary Care Monitor: structure, process and outcome indicators. *BMC Family Practice*, 11(81).

Kringos DS et al. (2010b). The breadth of primary care: a systematic literature review of its core dimensions. *BMC Health Service Research*, 10(1):65.

Kringos DS et al. (2013). Europe's strong primary care systems are linked to better population health but also to higher health spending. *Health Affairs*, 32(4):686–694.

Liseckiene I et al. (2007). Primary care in a post-communist country: comparison of service profiles of Lithuanian primary care physicians in 1994 and GPs in 2004. *Health Policy*, 83:105–113.

Macinko J, Starfield B, Shi L (2003). The contribution of primary care systems to health outcomes within Organisation for Economic Co-operation and Development (OECD), 1970–1998. *Health Service Research*, 38(3):831–865.

Mladovsky P et al. (2012). *Health policy responses to the financial crisis in Europe.* Copenhagen, WHO Regional Office for Europe, on behalf of the European Observatory on Health Systems and Policies (Policy summary 5).

Monteagudo Peña JL, Moreno Gil O (2007). *e-Health for patient empowerment in Europe.* Madrid, Instituto de Salud Carlos III.

Nolte E et al. (2008). *Managing chronic conditions: experience in eight countries.* Copenhagen, WHO Regional Office for Europe on behalf of the European Observatory on Health Systems and Policies.

OECD (2008). *International migration outlook: SOPEMI – 2008 edition.* Paris, Organisation for Economic Co-operation and Development.

Rechel B, McKee M (2009). Health reform in central and eastern Europe and the former Soviet Union. *The Lancet*, 374(9696):1186–1195.

Saltman RB, Rico A, Boerma WGW (2006). *Primary care in the driver's seat? Organizational reform in European primary care.* The European Observatory on Health Systems and Policy. Maidenhead, Open University Press.

Seifert B (2008). Perspectives of family medicine in central and eastern Europe. *Family Practice*, 25(2):113–18.

Starfield B (1992). *Primary care: concept, evaluation, and policy.* New York, Oxford University Press.

Starfield B (1994). Is primary care essential? *The Lancet*, 344:1129–1133.

Svab I et al. (2004). General practice east of Eden: an overview of general practice in eastern Europe. *Croatian Medical Journal*, 45(5):537–542.

WHO (2000). *World health report 2000. Health systems: improving performance.* Geneva, World Health Organization.

WHO (2008). *World health report 2008. Primary health care now more than ever.* Geneva, World Health Organization.

WHO Regional Office for Europe (2013). *WHO policy dialogue on international health workforce mobility and recruitment challenges: technical report.* Copenhagen, WHO Regional Office for Europe.

World Bank (2005). *Review of experience of family medicine in Europe and Central Asia, vol. 1.* Washington, DC, World Bank (World Bank, Report No. 32354-ECA).

Chapter 2

Structure and organization of primary care

Margus Lember, Thomas Cartier, Yann Bourgueil, Toni Dedeu,
Allen Hutchinson, Dionne Kringos

The way primary care is structured establishes important conditions for both the process of care and its outcomes. In this chapter, the structure of primary care will be discussed according to three dimensions: governance, economic conditions and workforce development. Governance refers to the vision and direction of health policy, which exerts influence through regulation and advocacy as well as through collecting and using information. The economic conditions of a primary care system are dominated by the total amount spent on it and how access to care for patients is organized financially. Cost-sharing, for instance, can be a source of inequity in financial access to care. The mode of remuneration of care providers is also a relevant economic condition. Primary care professionals can be salaried or self-employed and may or may not be contracted to health services or health insurance institutions. The dimension of workforce development refers to the professional profile of primary care workers and the role they play in the health care system. The chapter will conclude with a comparison of the governance, financing and workforce development conditions, and their interrelations, across European countries.

2.1 Governance

Governance, belonging to the dimensions of structure mentioned in the primary care framework (see chapter 1), involves a complex of features of policy implementation at different levels. The perspective taken in this chapter combines forms of governance with elements found in various definitions. The conceptual starting point is Keohane's (2002) definition of governance: "the set of principles, norms, roles, and decision-making procedures around which actors converge in a given public policy arena". Furthermore, concepts derived from regime theory are used, such as outcomes (in the form of quality management of infrastructures); the existence of a judicial support background (including laws and regulations); and the existence of administrative practices that constrain, prescribe or enable the provision of services (Frederickson, 2005). The translation of these definitions into a measurable tool has resulted in the selection of six features and various indicators, which provide a broad view of governance in primary care and allows comparisons to be made among the countries examined. The latter will be discussed in the next section. (Appendix I contains details of governance features, indicators and additional information items).

Table 2.1 provides an overview per country of selected results of the governance of primary care.

Vision on primary care

The availability of an explicit governmental vision on the role of primary care in the health care system is among the indicators of governance. A vision on current and future primary care has been identified as far as it has been explicitly laid down in policy documents. Such visions on primary care were not always available. They were poorly developed, in particular, in Austria, Belgium, the Czech Republic, Germany, Hungary, Iceland, Latvia, Poland, Slovakia, Sweden and Switzerland. In a number of countries visions were focused on (partial) reforms of the primary care system; this was the case in Cyprus, Finland, Ireland, Italy, Portugal and Romania.

In general, results show that countries with a gatekeeping system produce more formal governmental pro-primary care policies, and vice versa. Furthermore, the characteristics of the type of health system in the countries, such as social health insurance (SHI) or a national health service (NHS), were not found to be related to the extent that supportive primary care policies were in place.

Table 2.1

Governance of primary care system, overview of selection of results by country

Country	PC vision (Topics) [1]	Policy on equal distribution PC practices	Policy on multidisciplinary collaboration	PC unit at MoH	Specific PC budget	Decentralization of PC responsibilities (level)	Decentralized responsibilities	Stakeholder involvement PC policy level	Community influence on PC provision (level)	State inspection with PC unit	Requirements for practising in PC & PC facilities to operate	Evidence-based clinical guidelines for GPs (mode of production) [2]	Patient rights laws on [3]
Austria	No	Yes	No	No	No	Yes Regional SHI funds	Financing; Supply planning	Yes	Yes Incidentally at local level	Yes	P: Yes O: Yes	Yes GP; FOR; MED	IC; AC; CO; PR
Belgium	No	No	Yes	No	No	No	–	Yes	Yes Incidentally at local level	No	P: Yes O: No	Yes NAT; GP; MED	IC; AC; CO; PR
Bulgaria	Yes ACCREMA; GRP; MDW; NRS; QUALM; TRN; WRKL	Yes	Yes	No	Yes	Yes Reg. health centres; Reg. NHIF	Financing; Supply planning; Quality monitoring	Yes	Yes Incidentally at local level	Yes	P: Yes O: Yes	Yes NAT; GP; FOR; MED	IC; AC; CO; PR
Cyprus	Yes NWPCS; NWSTR	Yes	Yes	–	No	Yes Regional hospitals	Supply planning; Service provision; Priority setting	No	Yes Incidentally at local level	No	P: Yes O: No	Yes NAT; FOR; MED	IC; CO
Czech Republic	No	No	No	No	No	Yes District authorities	Service provision	Yes	Yes At national level	No	P: Yes O: No	Yes GP	IC; AC; CO; PR
Denmark	Yes CHR; COLL; GRP; GTK; PRV	No	Yes	No	Yes	Yes Regions; Municipalities	Management and planning; Financing; Service provision; Quality development	Yes	Yes At national level	No	P: Yes O: No	Yes GP	IC; AC; CO; PR
Estonia	Yes ACC; COLL	Yes	Yes	No	Yes	No	–	Yes	Yes At national level	No	P: Yes O: No	Yes GP; FOR; MED	IC; AC; CO; PR
Finland	Yes CHR; NWSTR; PCDEV	No	Yes	No	Yes	Yes Municipalities	Management and planning; Financing; Service provision	Yes	Yes Regularly at local level	No	P: Yes O: No	Yes GP; MED	IC; AC; CO; PR
France	Yes ACC; CON; COO; COM; HEP; PHAR	Yes	No	No	No	Yes Regional health agencies	Financing; Supply planning; Service provision	Yes	Yes Incidentally at local level	No	P: Yes O: No	Yes NAT; MED	IC; AC; CO

Germany	No	Yes	No	No	No	Yes Reg. assocs; Statutory health insurance	Financing; Supply planning; Service provision	Yes	Yes Incidentally at local level	No	P: Yes O: No	Yes GP	IC; AC; CO; PR
Greece	Yes COM; HEP; PRV	No	–	Yes	Yes	Yes Regions	No info. available	Yes	Yes Incidentally at local level	–	P: Yes O: –	–	–
Hungary	No	No	No	No	Yes	No	–	No	No	No	P: Yes O: No	Yes GP	IC; AC; CO; PR
Iceland	No	No	No	No	Yes	Yes Regions; Municipalities	Financing; Service provision; Priority setting	Yes	–	No	P: – O: –	–	IC; CO; PR
Ireland	Yes COLL; NWSTR; NWPCS	Yes	Yes	Yes	Yes	Yes Regions; Local health offices	Supply planning; Service provision; Priority setting	Yes	Yes At national level	No	P: Yes O: No	No	IC; AC; PR
Italy	Yes COLL; NWSTR	Yes	Yes	No	Yes	Yes Regional governments	Financing; Supply planning; Service provision; Priority setting; Quality monitoring	No	Yes In some regions	Yes	P: Yes O: Yes	Yes NAT; GP; FOR; MED	IC; AC; CO; PR
Latvia	No	Yes	Yes	No	Yes	No	–	Yes	Yes At national level	No	P: Yes O: Yes	Yes MED	IC; AC; CO; PR
Lithuania	Yes DEN; MHC; NRS; PCDEV	No	Yes	Yes	Yes	Yes Municipalities	No info. available	Yes	Yes In some regions	No	P: Yes O: Yes	Yes GP; FOR; MED	IC; AC; CO; PR
Luxembourg	No	No	No	No	No	No	–	Yes	No	No	P: Yes O: Yes	Yes FOR; MED	AC; CO; PR
Malta	Yes CON; COM; DEC; PCDEV	Yes	–	Yes	No	No	–	Yes	No	No	P: Yes O: Yes	No	IC; AC; CO
Netherlands	Yes COLL; COP; ENTR; ICT; INN; NWSTR; PAT; PCDEV; TASK	Yes	Yes	Yes	No	Yes Municipalities	Service provision	Yes	Yes At national level	Yes	P: Yes O: Yes	Yes GP; FOR; MED	IC; AC; CO; PR
Norway	Yes COO; DEC	No	Yes	Yes	Yes	Yes Municipalities	Financing; Service provision; Priority setting; Quality monitoring	Yes	Yes At national level	No	P: Yes O: Yes	Yes NAT; MED	IC; AC; CO; PR
Poland	No	No	No	No	Yes	Yes Local authorities	Service provision; Quality monitoring	No	Yes In some regions	No	P: Yes O: Yes	Yes GP; FOR; MED	IC; AC; CO; PR

Portugal	Yes ACC; CON; EFF; NWSTR; QUA; SAT	Yes	Yes	Yes	Yes	Yes Health regions	Financing; Service provision	Yes	Yes In some regions	No	P: Yes O: Yes	Yes NAT; GP; FOR	IC; AC; CO; PR
Romania	Yes ACCREMA; COLL; COM; DEC; ICT; NRS; NWSTR; PCDEV; PRINFR; PRIV; QUALM; WRKF	Yes	Yes	No	Yes	Yes District health directorates	Financing; Service provision; Priority setting	Yes	Yes Incidentally at local level	No	P: Yes O: Yes	Yes NAT; GP; MED	IC; AC; CO; PR
Slovakia	No	No	No	No	No	No	–	No	No	n.a.	P: Yes O: Yes	Yes GP	IC; AC; CO; PR
Slovenia	Yes COO; COLL; NRS; QUA; QUALM; WRKF	Yes	Yes	No	Yes	Yes Local communities	Policy development; Supply planning; Service provision	Yes	Yes Incidentally at local level	No	P: Yes O: Yes	Yes GP; FOR; MED	IC; AC; CO; PR
Spain	Yes COLL; GTK; HEP; PCDEV; PRV	Yes	Yes	No	Yes	Yes Autonomous communities	Policy development; Supply planning; Financing; Service provision	Yes	Yes In some regions	Yes	P: Yes O: Yes	Yes GP	IC; AC; CO; PR
Sweden	No	Yes	Yes	No	No	Yes Counties	Policy development; Supply planning; Financing; Service provision	Yes	Yes In some regions	No	P: Yes O: Yes	Yes GP; FOR; MED	IC; AC; CO; PR
Switzerland	No	No	No	No	No	No	–	Yes	Yes In some regions	No	P: Yes O: Yes	No	AC; CO
Turkey	Yes ACC; ACCREMA; MEDR; QUALM; TASK; TRN; WRKF	No	No	Yes	Yes	Yes Provincial health directorates	Supply planning; Service provision	Yes	Yes Incidentally at local level	No	P: Yes O: Yes	Yes NAT; MED	IC; AC; CO; PR
United Kingdom	Yes ACCREMA; COLL; COM; COMPE; PAT; QUAL; TASK	Yes	Yes	No	Yes	Yes PCTs; Health boards	Financing; Priority setting; Service provision	Yes	Yes At national level	No	P: Yes O: Yes	Yes NAT; MED	IC; AC; CO; PR

1 ACC = Access in general; ACCREMA = Access remote areas; CHR = Chronically ill people; COLL = Multidisciplinary collaboration of care; COM = Comprehensiveness of PC services; COMPE = Competitive health care market; CON = Continuity of care; COO = Coordination of care; COP = Co-payment system; DEC = Decentralization of the health care system; DEN = Dentistry; EFF = Efficiency of health care; ENTR = Entrepreneurship in health care; GRP = Group practices; GTK = Gatekeeping function of general practice; HEP = Health education and promotion; ICT = The use of Information and Communication Technologies; INN = Innovation in health care; MDW = midwifery care; MEDR = Medical record keeping; MHC = Mental health care; NRS = Nursing care; NWPCS = Creating a PC-driven health care system reform; NWSTR = Creating new PC structures, such as PC practices, or health care centres; PAT = Patient centredness and involvement; PCDEV = Development of PC in general; PRINFR = The infrastructure of PC practices or centres; PRIV = Private sector; PRV = Preventive care; PHAR = Pharmaceutical care and products; QUALM = Quality monitoring; QUA = Quality of care in general; SAT = Satisfaction of health care professionals and/or users; TASK = Task profile of PC workers; TRN = Training and (re-)accreditation of workforce; WRKF = Workforce capacity planning and development; WRKL = Workload.

2 NAT = Issued by a national agency such as the Ministry of Health; GP = Issued by a college or association of GPs; FOR = Adapted foreign guidelines; MED = Developed by medical specialists.

3 IC = Informed consent; AC = Patient access to own medical files; CO = Confidential use of medical records; PR = Availability of procedure to process patient complaints in PC facilities.

One of the most consistent policy characteristics in countries with strong primary care is the governments' attempts to distribute resources equitably and avoid inequalities.

Central, regional and local responsibilities for primary care

In a relatively small number of countries, including Estonia, Hungary, Latvia, Malta, Slovakia and Switzerland, responsibilities for primary care have been centralized at national level. In other countries essential functions, such as priority setting, financing, supply planning and management, provision of services or quality monitoring are the responsibility of regional or local authorities or regional health insurance funds, hospitals or primary care trusts. Countries where the most functions in primary care have been decentralized are Denmark, Italy, Norway, Spain and Sweden. In Malta, Norway and Romania (further) decentralization of primary care has been included as a system target. A possible disadvantage of decentralization is the existence of inequalities in policies, and eventually in access to and quality of primary care. Some countries where important responsibilities for primary care have been decentralized have national policies to ensure an even distribution of providers and services. Such explicit national policies are not in place, however, in the Czech Republic, Finland, Greece, Iceland, Norway, Poland and Turkey.

Promoting responsiveness and quality of care

Responsiveness of health care systems can be facilitated either through stakeholder involvement in policy development or by community participation in the organization and provision of services. In most countries stakeholders and the community are involved in some way in these issues. In Cyprus, Italy, Luxembourg and Malta only one form occurs, while neither one occurs in Hungary and Slovakia.

Aspects of patient rights, such as informed consent for treatment, the possibility of patients having access to their own medical records, regulation on confidential use of medical records and the availability of patient complaint procedures in primary care facilities have a legal basis in all countries except Cyprus, France, Iceland, Ireland, Luxembourg, Malta and Switzerland. The least protected patient right in these countries is the availability of patient complaint procedures.

Quality assurance by means of formal medical educational requirements for providers to work in primary care is in place in all countries. However, Cyprus, Finland and Hungary are more lenient with these requirements in times of shortages of supply, allowing nonspecialized physicians to practise in primary care. In addition to personal educational requirements to practise, in most countries primary care facilities need permission to operate. Such permissions are not required, however, in Belgium, Finland, France, Germany, Ireland, Luxembourg and Norway.

Quality assurance through the development of evidence-based clinical guidelines for GPs exists in all countries except Ireland, Malta and Switzerland. Usually such guidelines have been produced by a combination of stakeholders, including ministries of health, a college or association of GPs and medical specialists. Sometimes foreign guidelines are used and adapted for the national situation.

Overall governance of primary care by country

Fig. 2.1 provides an overview of the overall scores on primary care governance by country, showing the performance of each country on all indicators that have been used on the governance dimension. Details on the scoring system can be found in Appendix II.

The figure shows that in most countries governance structures aiming to enhance the commitment towards primary care are relatively well developed. Furthermore, consistency among countries can be identified in the scores on the various indicators.

Three variables of (state-related) governance turn out to be weakly developed. In only eight countries is there a specific unit responsible for primary care within the Ministry of Health, while five countries have a state inspectorate to maintain the quality of care. Besides, in one-third of the countries no governmental policy on multidisciplinary collaboration could be identified.

The results show that countries with a gatekeeping system have a stronger primary care orientation in their governance than those without (Pearson correlation of 0.64; *p*-value 0.00).

Despite the modest variation in primary care governance scores across Europe, two contrasting groups of countries can be identified. Among the countries with strong primary care governance are: the Netherlands, Spain, the United Kingdom, Portugal, Italy, Denmark, Norway, Slovenia, Romania, Estonia, and Lithuania. The group of countries with weakest primary care governance consists of Switzerland, Cyprus, Luxembourg, Hungary, Iceland, Malta, the Slovakia, Ireland, and Poland. The other countries hold an intermediate position on primary care governance.

Fig. 2.1

Total governance of primary care score by country
(scale 1 (low) – 3 (high))

2.2 Economic conditions

Economic conditions of primary care, which is the second structure dimension in the framework, are largely determined by the proportion of total health expenditures spent on primary care and the financial conditions for access to care for patients. Cost-sharing and co-payment can threaten equity in financial access to care. Furthermore, financial incentives for health care workers can play a role. Primary care professionals can be salaried or self-employed providers, either contracted or not to the health services or health insurance system. The employment status and mode of remuneration may also influence the attractiveness of primary care professions.

The next section will discuss the four features of the economic conditions of primary care (see Appendix I for an overview of the features and indicators). Table 2.2 provides an overview of results of the economic conditions of primary care by country.

Primary care expenditure

Primary care expenditure strongly varies among countries. To some extent this results from the services included in the expenditures for primary care. A uniform methodology for calculating primary care expenditure across countries is not available and this hampers the comparability of this indicator. For example, in some countries it is limited to costs for family practice only, while in others freely accessible specialist care services are also included. Additionally, costs for community nursing, primary mental health care, dentistry and emergency care may be included in primary care costs. Even in family practice fund-holding, elements for laboratory tests and other investigations can be included. Finally, uniformity in the allocation of costs of prescribed medicines is absent.

Given these reservations, for 21 of 31 countries a comparison can be presented on primary care expenditure. In these countries the share varied from 4.7% in the Czech Republic to 25.6% in Switzerland. The share of prevention and public health expenditure varied from 0.6% in Cyprus to 18.4% in the Netherlands. It is difficult to draw comparisons from these data because of the wide variability in calculating expenditure.

Primary care benefits package

In general, the coverage of the population for medical expenses is quite comprehensive. In half of the countries coverage for primary care costs is complete, while most of the other half have coverage close to that. There are two exceptions: Cyprus with 80% and Ireland with 33%. For Turkey no exact data on coverage were available. In most countries the coverage for prescribed medicines is close to the coverage for primary care costs in general, with the exception of Bulgaria, where the coverage for prescribed medicines is 40%. No data were available for Romania and Turkey. In Cyprus the coverage for medicines is complete, and thus better than the overall coverage for primary care services.

Employment status of GPs

Countries differ in the dominant employment status of primary care providers, in particular GPs. In the following 18 countries GPs are predominantly self-employed: Belgium, Bulgaria, the Czech Republic, Denmark, Estonia, Germany, Hungary, Ireland, Italy, Latvia, Luxembourg, the Netherlands, Norway, Romania, Slovakia, Switzerland, Turkey and the United Kingdom. In these countries the large majority of self-employed GPs usually have contracts with health insurance or a health authority.

In Finland, Iceland, Lithuania, Poland, Portugal, Slovenia, Spain and Sweden all or most GPs are salaried either with the national, regional or local authorities or by other GPs. In most of these countries health care is funded through governmental budgets, not by health insurance. Countries with salaried GPs often offer them the possibility to work part-time in private practice.

The payment scheme of independently working GPs is usually a mix of capitation and fee-for-service payment. Fee-for-service payment is only reported for Cyprus, France and Switzerland. In half of the countries with salaried GPs these have a flat salary while in the other half the salary is combined with pay-for-performance elements and related to the number of patients served.

The comparison of annual income of GPs is complex as different components are included in the overall income in the countries. In some countries practice costs, practice staff costs and even costs for laboratory expenses are included. In countries where the data do not include practice costs, the average estimated annual income of a GP ranges from €10 782 in Lithuania to €150 000 in Luxembourg. In the group of countries where the data include practice costs, it varies from €13 688 in Bulgaria to €71 514 in Belgium. Comparisons of net incomes are even more difficult as taxation systems strongly differ.

As the level of funding of health care and primary care in a country are related to indicators of economic development, it is not surprising that, in general, in countries with a high gross domestic product (GDP) GPs have relatively high incomes as well. However, there are other determinants of the income of GPs, as the different income positions of GPs in the high-GDP countries Belgium and the United Kingdom show.

Table 2.2

Economic conditions of primary care, overview of selection of results by country

Country	Average gross annual income of GPs in EUR [/year] (incl. = incl. practice costs)	Remuneration system for self-employed GPs	Remuneration system for salaried GPs	Decentralization of PC responsibilities (level): self-employed without contract (paid by patients out-of-pocket)	self-employed with contract to health insurance fund(s) or health authority	salaried with other physicians	salaried with nat., reg. or local authorities
Austria	90 852.98[05]	Mix of capitation, FFS & other components	Flat salary	29.1	20.4	–	49.0
Belgium	71 514.00[09] (incl.)	Mix of capitation, FFS & other components	Flat salary	–	99.7	0.3	–
Bulgaria	13 688.51[09] (incl.)	Mix of capitation, FFS & other components	Flat salary	–	86.6	13.4	–
Cyprus	55 000.00[09]	FFS payment	Flat salary	50.0	–	–	50.0
Czech Republic	25 000.00[10]	Mix of capitation & FFS	Flat salary	–	95.0	4.0	1.0
Denmark	135 000.00[10]	Mix of capitation & FFS	–	–	100		
Estonia	17 500.00[08]	Mix of capitation, FFS & other components	Flat salary	–	95.0	5.0	–
Finland	64 253.79[07]	–	Salary related to both patients nr. & perform. indicators	–	–	–	100
France	125 659.00[06]	FFS payment (optional P4P)	Flat salary	0.2	59.8		31.7
Germany	84 300.00[07]	Mix of capitation & FFS	Flat salary	–	87.0	10.0	3.0
Greece	25 000.00[09] (–)	FFS payment	Flat salary		50.0		50.0
Hungary	35 500.00[10] (incl.)	Mix of capitation, FFS & other components	Flat salary	–	95.0	1.0	4.0
Iceland	70 000.00[09]	FFS payment	Flat salary	5.0	5.0	–	90.0

Country	% pop. insured for medicines prescribed in PC	% population insured for PC costs	% population uninsured for medical expenses	Prevention & public health expenditure as % of total HE [/year]	PC expenditure as % of total HE [/year]
Austria	98.0	98.0	2.0	1.8[07]	–
Belgium	99.0	99.0	<1	3.9[07]	19.0[10]
Bulgaria	35–40	95.0	5–10	3.5[06]	6.0[10]
Cyprus	100	80.0	10.0	0.6[06]	10.0[10]
Czech Republic	100	100	0	2.2[07]	4.7[07]
Denmark	100	98.0	0	1.4[07]	–
Estonia	95.6	95.6	4.4	2.6[07]	7.1[09]
Finland	100	100	0	5.4[07]	–
France	94.55	94.6	0.1	2.6[08]	19.3[10]
Germany	99.8	99.8	0.2	4.0[08]	–
Greece	–	100	–	–	22.9[97]
Hungary	100	100	<1	2.4[10]	10.3[10]
Iceland	–	100	5.0	0.7[10]	–

Ireland	13.0[09]	3.5[05]	50.0	33.0	30.0	–	–	80.0	20.0	–	Mix of capitation & FFS	110 000.00[09]
Italy	5.7[08]	3.6[07]	5.0	100	100	–	–	100	–	–	Mix of capitation, FFS & other components	50 000.00[10] (incl.)
Latvia	9.7[09]	1.2[09]	0	100	100	8.0	–	90.0	2.0	Salary related to both patients nr. & perform. indicators	Mix of capitation, FFS & other components	45 000.00[08] (incl.)
Lithuania	13.8[09]	1.3[06]	5.0	99.0	95.0	80.0	–	19.0	1.0	Salary related to both patients nr. & perform. indicators	Mix of capitation & FFS	10 782.00[09]
Luxembourg	–	1.1[05]	2.1	97.9	100	10.0	–	90.0	–	Flat salary	FFS payment	150 000.00[08]
Malta	–	–	–	100	100	35.0	–		65.0	Flat salary	FFS payment	10.808,30[99] (–)
Netherlands	14.7[08]	18.4[05]	1.0	99.0	99.0		15.0	85.0	–	Flat salary	Mix of capitation & FFS	112 464.90[06]
Norway	5.8[08]	1.9[08]	0	100	100	7.0	–	93.0	–	Flat salary	Mix of capitation & FFS	115 000.00[10] (incl.)
Poland	13.3[09]	2.2[07]	2.3	97.7	97.7	76.0		24.0		Flat salary	Mix of capitation & FFS	38 400.00[09] (incl.)
Portugal	–	1.8[06]	0	100	100	99.0	1.0	–	–	Salary related to both patients nr. & perform. indicators	–	60 000.00[09]
Romania	10.2[08]	5.9[06]	0	100	–	–	24.0	–	76.0	Salary related to both patients nr. & perform. indicators	Mix of capitation & FFS	31 818.00[08] (incl.)
Slovakia	8.0[10]	4.5[06]	0	100	100	0.5	0.5	99.0	–	Flat salary	Mix of capitation, FFS & other components	12 000.00[09]
Slovenia	12.2[08]	4.1[06]	0.09	100	100	72.0	–	28.0	–	Salary related to both patients nr. & perform. indicators	Mix of capitation & FFS	44 877.00[08]
Spain	14.1[05]	2.2[07]	0	100	100	80.0	–	20.0	–	Salary related to both patients nr. & perform. indicators	Mix of capitation, FFS & other components	45 000.00[09]
Sweden	–	3.5[07]	0	100	100	Majority	–		–	Flat salary	–	54 870.00[10]
Switzerland	25.6[07]	2.3[07]	0.8	99.2	99.2	–	–	90.0>	–		FFS payment	126 006.00[05]
Turkey	–	2.3[00]	12.7	–	–	–	–	100	–		Mix of capitation, FFS & other components	27 000.00[10]
United Kingdom	19.9[07] (ENG)	4.0[07] (ENG)	0	100	100	20.0		73.0	–	Salary related to both patients nr. & perform. indicators	Mix of capitation, FFS & other components	133 000.00[07]

Overall economic conditions of primary care by country

Fig. 2.2 provides an overview of the total economic conditions of primary care scores by country, considering the performance of each country on all economic conditions indicators (see Appendix II for an overview of the features and indicators used for the scores). The figure shows that the general economic conditions of primary care are most favourable in Belgium, Denmark, Finland, Germany, Italy, the Netherlands, Portugal, Slovenia, Spain and the United Kingdom. Countries where economic conditions for primary care are relatively poor are Bulgaria, Cyprus, the Czech Republic, Greece, Iceland, Ireland, Malta, Romania, Sweden and Turkey.

The variation between countries in the overall economic conditions of primary care is limited; scores range from 1.90 in Bulgaria to 2.26 in the United Kingdom. Still, there seems to be room for improvement in some countries on specific indicators. The expenditure on primary care, for instance, is relatively low in Bulgaria, the Czech Republic, Estonia, Italy, Latvia, Norway and Slovakia. Another point is that in 10 out of 31 countries primary care expenditure data could not be identified in the total health expenditures. Concerning the income of providers, a major observation is the considerable gap in most countries between the financial status of primary care providers compared to hospital specialists. The only countries where GPs have a financial status comparable to medical specialists are Cyprus, the Czech Republic, Hungary, Ireland, Portugal, Spain and the United Kingdom. In all other countries, the income of GPs is, usually considerably, lower than the income of most medical specialists. However, in these countries GPs earn considerably more than nurses and allied health care professionals.

No significant relationship was found between the national income (GDP) of countries and their overall economic conditions of primary care. This suggests that the financial policies and mechanisms applied are of greater influence than the financial resources available.

Fig. 2.2

Total economic conditions of primary care score by country
(scale 1 (low) – 3 (high))

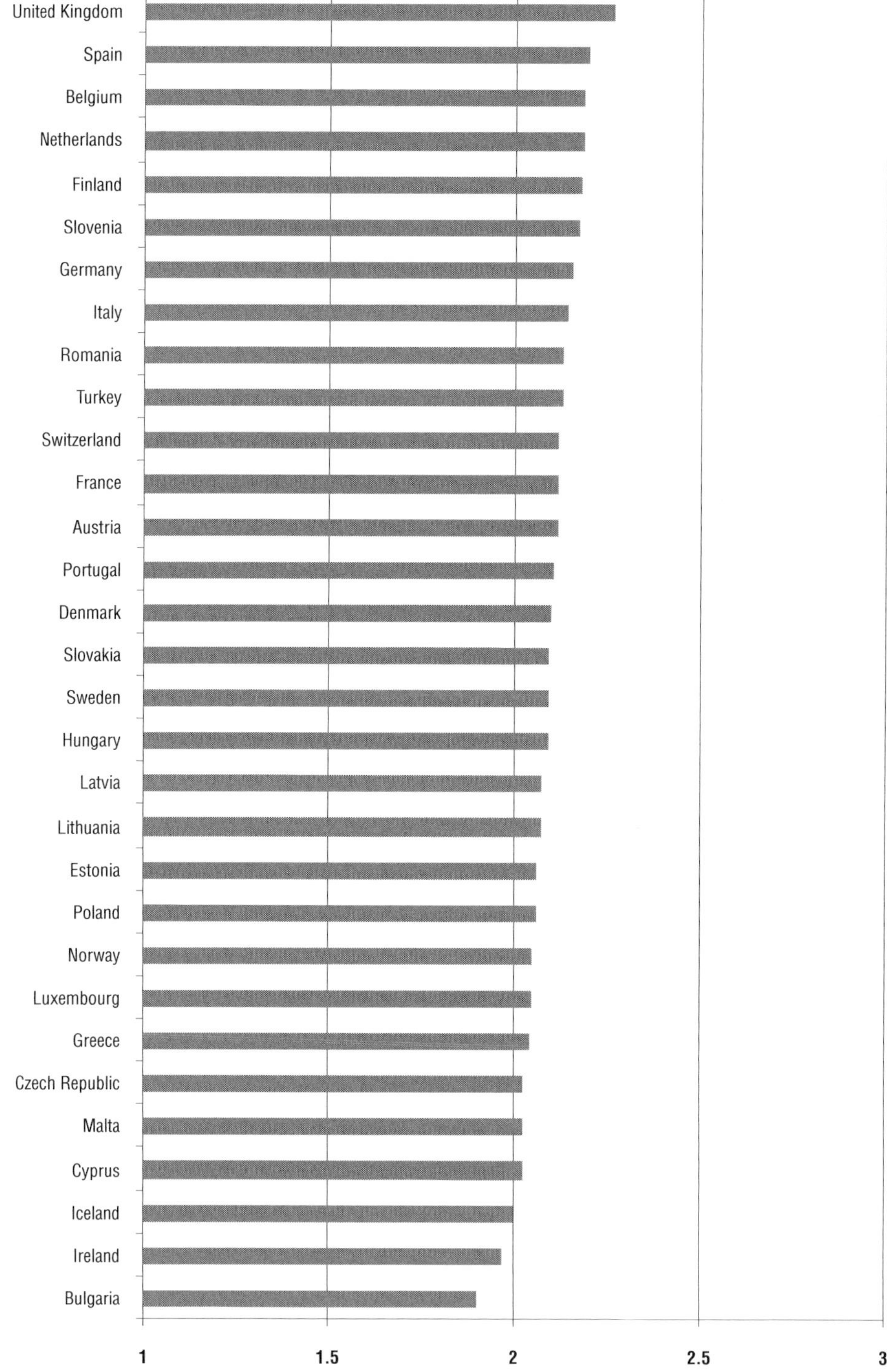

2.3 Workforce development

Workforce development, the third dimension of governance in the framework, refers to the profile of professionals providing primary care services and their position in the health care system. Important elements are, for example, the type of health care workers involved in primary care; their gender and age structure; and their professional recognition among other (medical) professions. For future continuity of GPs and other disciplines in primary care, the availability and quality of vocational training schemes, maintenance of an attractive profession and retention of workers are important. Being prepared for future workforce needs implies quantitative and qualitative capacity planning.

Professional development and defence of the interests of primary care workers can largely be attributed to academic departments, professional colleges and associations. Facilitated by governments these can also be involved in quality assurance, research and continuing medical education. These features will be discussed in the next section for each of the countries (see Appendix I for an overview of the features and indicators applied).

Table 2.3 provides an overview of results of the primary care workforce development by country.

Table 2.3

Primary care workforce development, overview of selection of results by country

Country	PC providers [1]	% of practising GPs aged 55+ years	Average nr of working hrs/wk of GPs	GP task profile is formally described	GP income level compared to most specialists' income	% change in supply of GPs over 5 yrs time average for all PC providers	PC workforce capacity planning in place	Family medicine is subject in undergraduate medical training	% med. universities with postgraduate FM / GP training (Year of introduction)	Professional training for district nurses & PC practice nurses [2]	Publication of a journal on FM/GP & PC nursing [2]
Austria	GP/FP; OB/GYN; PAED; INT; OPH; ENT; CAR; NEU; SUR; PCN; SPN; HCN; PHT; MID; OCT; SPCH; DEN	45.0	60	Yes	(Much) Lower	+10.8 +14.9 (2003– 2007)	No	Yes	0	DN: Yes PN: Yes	FM: No PN: No
Belgium	GP/FP; OB/GYN; PAED; INT; OPH; ENT; CAR; NEU; SUR; PCN; MID; DEN	39.1	49	No	Much lower	+0.7 +6.1 (2004– 2008)	Yes	Yes	80.0 (–)	DN: Yes PN: No	FM: Yes PN: Yes
Bulgaria	GP/FP; OB/GYN; PAED; DEN	15.0	36	Yes	(Much) Lower	-3.1 -1.7 (2002– 2006)	No	Yes	66.6 (1998)	DN: No PN: No	FM: Yes PN: No
Cyprus	GP/FP; OB/GYN; PAED; INT; OPH; ENT; CAR; NEU; SUR; PCN; SPN; DEN	55.0	–	No	Equal (public sector)	-20.4 +16.2 (1995– 2000)	No	No	0	DN: Yes PN: No	FM: – PN: –
Czech Republic	GP/FP; OB/GYN; PAED; OPH; ENT; CAR; SUR; PCN; PHT; DEN	65.8 (50+ yrs)	40	No	Equal	-1.9 +11.4 (2003– 2007)	No	Yes	0	DN: No PN: No	FM: Yes PN: No
Denmark	GP/FP; OB/GYN; PAED; INT; OPH; ENT; CAR; NEU; SUR; PHT; DEN	51.0	44	Yes	Much lower	+4.3 +8.0 (2002– 2006)	Yes	Yes	75.0 (1985)	DN: Yes PN: Yes	FM: Yes PN: Yes
Estonia	GP/FP; OB/GYN; OPH; PCN; MID; OCT; DEN	38.8	40	Yes	(Much) Lower	+12.4 +54.9 (2002– 2006)	Yes	Yes	100.0 (1991)	DN: No PN: Yes	FM: Yes PN: No
Finland	GP/FP; PCN; SPN; HCN; PHT; MID; OCT; SPCH; DEN	–	40	No	(Much) Lower	+12.8 +7.3 (1999– 2003)	No	Yes	100.0 (1961)	DN: Yes PN: Yes	FM: Yes PN: No
France	GP/FP; OB/GYN; PAED; OPH; ENT; CAR; NEU; SUR; PHT; MID; OCT; SPCH; DEN	32.9	49	Yes	(Much) Lower	-0.5 +4.4 (2004– 2008)	Yes	No	100.0 (1988)	DN: No PN: No	FM: Yes PN: No

Germany	GP/FP; OB/GYN; PAED; INT; OPH; ENT; CAR; NEU; SUR; MID; DEN	42.9 (50+ yrs)	51	Yes	(Much) Lower	-6.0 +7.0 (2002–2006)	Yes	Yes	0	DN: No PN: Yes	FM: Yes PN: No
Greece	GP/FP; OB/GYN; PAED; INT; OPH; ENT; CAR; NEU; SUR; PCN; SPN	–	50	Yes	(Much) Lower	+36.1 +12.1 (2001–2005)	Yes	Yes	50.0 (1986)	DN: No PN: No	FM: Yes PN: No
Hungary	GP/FP; OB/GYN; PAED; OPH; ENT; SUR; PCN; MID; DEN	48.0	35	Yes	Equal/ Lower	-2.2 -9.8 (2002–2006)	No	Yes	100.0 (1999)	DN: Yes PN: Yes	FM: Yes PN: No
Iceland	GP/FP; OB/GYN; PAED; INT; OPH; ENT; CAR; NEU; SUR; PCN; SPN; HCN; PHT; MID; OCT; SPCH; DEN	32.0	43	No	Lower	+11.5 +9.4 (1998–2001)	No	Yes	100.0 (1990)	DN: Yes PN: No	FM: No PN: No
Ireland	GP/FP; OB/GYN; PAED; INT; OPH; ENT; CAR; NEU; SUR; PCN; HCN; PHT; MID; OCT; SPCH; DEN	31.0	40	No	Equal	+17.4 +23.7 (2004–2006)	Yes	Yes	100.0 (1972)	DN: Yes PN: No	FM: Yes PN: Yes
Italy	GP/FP; OB/GYN; PAED; OPH; CAR; HCN; PHT; SPCH; DEN	87.0 (50+ yrs)	39	Yes	Lower	+0.12 +81.8 (2002–2007)	–	Yes	0	DN: Yes PN: No	FM: Yes PN: No
Latvia	GP/FP; OB/GYN; PAED; OPH; PCN; MID; DEN	27.0	40	Yes	(Much) Lower	+18.8 -4.2 (2003–2007)	No	Yes	100.0 (1993)	DN: No PN: No	FM: No PN: No
Lithuania	GP/FP; OB/GYN; PAED; SUR; PCN; DEN	25.0	38	Yes	Lower	+43.1 +3.6 (2002–2006)	Yes	Yes	100.0 (1993)	DN: Yes PN: Yes	FM: Yes PN: No
Luxembourg	GP/FP; OB/GYN; PAED; INT; OPH; ENT; CAR; NEU; SUR; HCN; MID; DEN	32.0	60	Yes	Much lower	+5.5 +11.2 (2003–2008)	No	No	100.0 (2004)	DN: No PN: No	FM: No PN: No
Malta	GP/FP; OB/GYN; PAED; PCN; MID; DEN	11.0	44	–	Lower	+1.6 +5.4 (1998–2007)	–	Yes	100.0 (2005)	DN: – PN: –	FM: Yes PN: –
Netherlands	GP/FP; PCN; SPN; HCN; PHT; MID; OCT; DEN	27.6	44	Yes	Much lower	+5.4 +21.7 (2004–2009)	Yes	Yes	100.0 (1974)	DN: No PN: Yes	FM: Yes PN: Yes
Norway	GP/FP; HCN; PHT; MID; OCT; DEN	51.0 (50+ yrs)	49	Yes	–	+11.4 +8.6 (2002–2006)	Yes	Yes	100.0 (1985)	DN: No PN: No	FM: Yes PN: No

58 Building primary care in a changing Europe

Poland	GP/FP; OB/GYN; PAED; INT; OPH; PCN; MID; DEN	–	50	Yes	Equal/ Lower	+27.2 -4.5 (2003– 2006)	No	Yes	91.6 (1994)	DN: No PN: Yes	FM: Yes PN: No
Portugal	GP/FP; PCN	18.0	42	Yes	Equal	+6.1 +6.1 (2001– 2005)	Yes	Yes	100.0 (1981)	DN: Yes PN: No	FM: Yes PN: No
Romania	GP/FP; PCN; HCN; PHT; MID; OCT	–	48	No	Lower	+22.7 +7.6 (2005– 2006)	No	Yes	100.0 (1990)	DN: Yes PN: Yes	FM: Yes PN: No
Slovakia	GP/FP; OB/GYN; PAED; OPH; DEN	35.0	40	Yes	Much lower	-16.7 -10.2 (2002– 2006)	No	Yes	11.0 (1978)	DN: No PN: No	FM: Yes PN: No
Slovenia	GP/FP; OB/GYN; PAED; PCN; HCN; PHT; MID; DEN	33.5	40	No	Lower	+38.0 +28.5 (2002– 2006)	Yes	Yes	–	DN: – PN: –	FM: Yes PN: No
Spain	GP/FP; OB/GYN; PAED; PCN; HCN; MID; DEN	60.5 (50+ yrs)	40	Yes	Equal	+8.3 +14.8 (2003– 2007)	Yes	No	0 (1978)	DN: Yes PN: Yes	FM: Yes PN: Yes
Sweden	GP/FP; OB/GYN; PAED; INT; OPH; ENT; CAR; NEU; SUR; PCN; SPN; HCN; PHT; MID; OCT; SPCH	–	–	–	–	+9.6 +9.5 (2002– 2006)	Yes	Yes	–	DN: Yes PN: No	FM: Yes PN: –
Switzerland	GP/FP; OB/GYN; PAED; INT; OPH; ENT; CAR; NEU; SUR; PCN; PHT; MID; OCT; SPCH; DEN	43.0	44	No	(Much) Lower	-1.0 +4.3 (2004– 2008)	Yes	Yes	100.0 (–)	DN: Yes PN: No	FM: Yes PN: No
Turkey	GP/FP; OB/GYN; PAED; INT; OPH; ENT; CAR; NEU; SUR; PCN; SPN; HCN; PHT; MID; OCT; SPCH; DEN	1.3 (data from[2] provinces)	51	Yes	(Much) Lower	-29.7 +17.5 (2004– 2008)	Yes	No	74.0 (1993)	DN: Yes PN: No	FM: Yes PN: No
United Kingdom	GP/FP; PCN; SPN; HCN; MID; DEN	30.0 (50+ yrs)	44	Yes	Equal	+9.1 +10.0 (2003– 2007)	Yes	Yes	0 (1951)	DN: Yes PN: Yes	FM: Yes PN: Yes

1 GP/FP = GP/Family Physician; OB/GYN = Obstetrician/Gynaecologist; PAED = Paediatrician; INT = Specialist of Internal medicine; OPH = Ophthalmologist; ENT = Ear Nose Throat Specialist; CAR = Cardiologist; NEU = Neurologist; SUR = Surgeon; PCN = Primary care/General practice nurse; SPN = Specialized nurse; HCN = Home care nurse; PHT = Physiotherapist (ambulatory); MID = Midwife (ambulatory); OCT = Occupational therapist; SPCH = Speech therapist; DEN = Dentist.
2 DN = District or community nurses; PN = Primary care/General practice nurses; FM=family medicine, general practice.

Professions active in primary care

The only primary care professionals that were found in each of the 31 countries included in this study are GPs, also referred to as family physicians. On average there are 68 GPs per 100 000 population in Europe, although the variation is very large. The contrast between the neighbouring countries Belgium and the Netherlands is very large. In the Netherlands, the number of GPs per 100 000 population is 47, while there are 115 per 100 000 in Belgium. Also dentists belong to primary care in most (27) countries. Also quite common in primary care are nurses; they are a regular discipline in 23 countries. However, nurses may have quite different roles in primary care, varying from specific nursing tasks, for instance with chronic patients, to more general support tasks. Specialized nurses and home care nurses are less prevalent as part of the primary care workforce (in almost half of the countries only). In 22 countries midwives are working in primary care.

Furthermore, in many countries patients have direct access to a number of medical specialties, and so these are also part of primary care. In two-thirds of the countries gynaecologists, paediatricians and ophthalmologists are considered as primary care professions. In about half of the countries specialists of internal medicine, ENT specialists, cardiologists, neurologists and surgeons are active as primary care providers.

Availability of GPs

Ageing among GPs may become a problem in many countries. In well over half of the countries studies are available or institutes are working on primary care demography and future capacity needs. With the exception of Turkey, where the average age is 39 years, GPs in the remaining countries are mostly between 45 and 55 years. Again, the age distribution varies strongly from one country to another. In countries like Cyprus, the Czech Republic, Italy, Norway, Spain and Sweden around half of the general practice workforce is over 55 years old. Countries seem to react differently to the imminent effects of the ageing of their GPs. In some countries the number of GPs has strongly increased in recent years, such as in Greece, Lithuania, Poland and Slovenia, while in others the numbers are decreasing steadily, for instance in Germany and Slovakia.

In addition to the age structure of the profession, workforce capacity is also related to the opening hours of practices and working hours of staff. The opening hours of general practices across Europe, excluding possible hours on-call, vary from 35 hours per week in Hungary to 100 hours per week in rural Austria. The average is 44 hours a week. These hours include both direct patient care and other activities. In some countries opening hours are subject to mandatory regulation, which also applies to GPs who are self-employed and work in their own practice.

Professional and academic status

The professional status of general practice has been identified through several indicators. The first is the existence of an official job description, either on a legal basis or in a professional code. This is the case in 20 countries in Europe. Fifteen countries have established a job description by law; most did so in the last 15 years. In Austria, Germany and the United Kingdom the tasks and duties of GPs are included in the contract between the financing body and the GP, while in Lithuania and Luxembourg job descriptions have been established by the professionals themselves. A second indicator of professional status is income level. With the exception of Portugal, Spain and the United Kingdom, which have NHS-type health care systems, GPs earn less or much less than medical specialists (although paediatricians and internists sometimes earn the same as GPs). However, if earnings of GPs are compared to those of other professions in primary care, such as specialized and home care nurses, physiotherapists, midwives, occupational and speech therapists, they always earn more to much more. In some countries dentists seem to earn more than GPs, while in others it is the other way around.

The attractiveness of general practice or primary care is also reflected in the preference of medical students choosing to become a GP or family physician. Except for Austria and France, around 17% of medical students throughout Europe choose to become GPs. In Austria, the rate is high because all physicians start off as GPs, before specialization to become a medical specialist. In France the rate is high because the number of positions in each medical specialty is determined by law and allocated according to the results of a mandatory ranking examination.

The situation of nurse training, specifically for primary care, varies. Eight countries offer no such training at all. In 13 countries nurses can specialize either to become a community nurse or a primary care practice nurse. In eight countries both specializations are possible.

Professional associations

In nearly all countries there is at least one professional organization for GPs, either an association or a college of GPs. Mostly they are involved in scientific, educational and professional development (guidelines, continuing medical education). Frequently, GPs also need to register with a physician's register, including all specialties.

Professional organizations for primary care nurses are rarer. Associations or organizations of primary care nurses exist in only 10 of 23 countries where primary care nurses are working. In most European countries a journal on family medicine is published, but not all of them are peer-reviewed or even have at least 50% of scientific content. On primary care nursing only six journals are available.

Overall primary care workforce development by country

Fig. 2.3 shows the total primary care workforce development scores by country, considering the performance of each country on all workforce development indicators (see Appendix II for an overview of the features and indicators used for the scores).

Compared to the governance and economic conditions of primary care, differences in workforce development of primary care are larger. They range from 1.62 in Iceland to 2.34 in the United Kingdom.

Relatively high levels of primary care workforce development are found in Denmark, Finland, Ireland, Malta, the Netherlands, Portugal, Slovenia, Spain, Switzerland and the United Kingdom. Workforce development is relatively low in Cyprus, the Czech Republic, Greece, Iceland, Latvia, Luxembourg, Malta, Poland, Slovakia, Slovenia and Sweden.

2.4 Overall structure of primary care

Fig. 2.4 summarizes the three dimensions of primary care structure – governance, economic conditions and workforce development – presented in this chapter. Each dimension has been depicted as an axis in the figure. With each pair of dimensions (governance + workforce development; governance + economic conditions; workforce development + economic conditions) the position of a country has been visualized: the darker the shade of green, the stronger the position of a country is.

Countries with a strong primary care structure (including governance, economic conditions and workforce development) are: Denmark, Finland, Italy, the Netherlands, Portugal, Romania, Slovenia, Spain and the United Kingdom. A relatively weak primary care structure on the three dimensions is found in Bulgaria, Cyprus, the Czech Republic, Greece, Iceland, Luxembourg, Poland and Slovakia. No consistent patterns of primary care structure could be identified in Estonia, Norway and Switzerland.

Overall, however, countries are consistent in their positions on the three dimensions (Spearman's correlation values were 0.49 for governance and workforce development with economic conditions (p-value 0.01) and 0.55 (p-value 0·00) for governance–workforce development).

Fig. 2.3
Total primary care workforce development score by country
(scale 1 (low) – 3 (high))

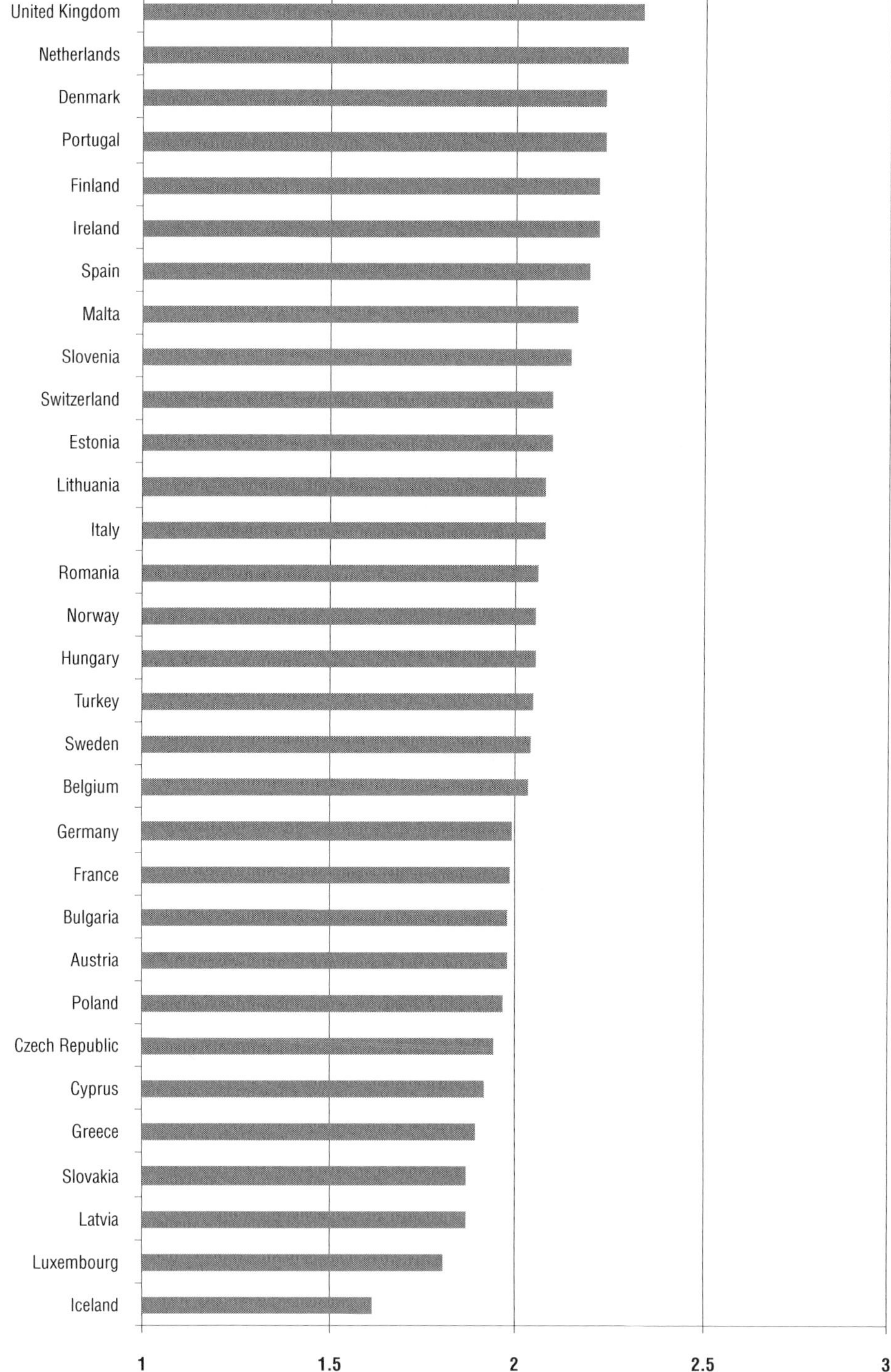

Fig. 2.4

Overall (high/medium/low) level of the governance, workforce development and economic conditions of primary care by country

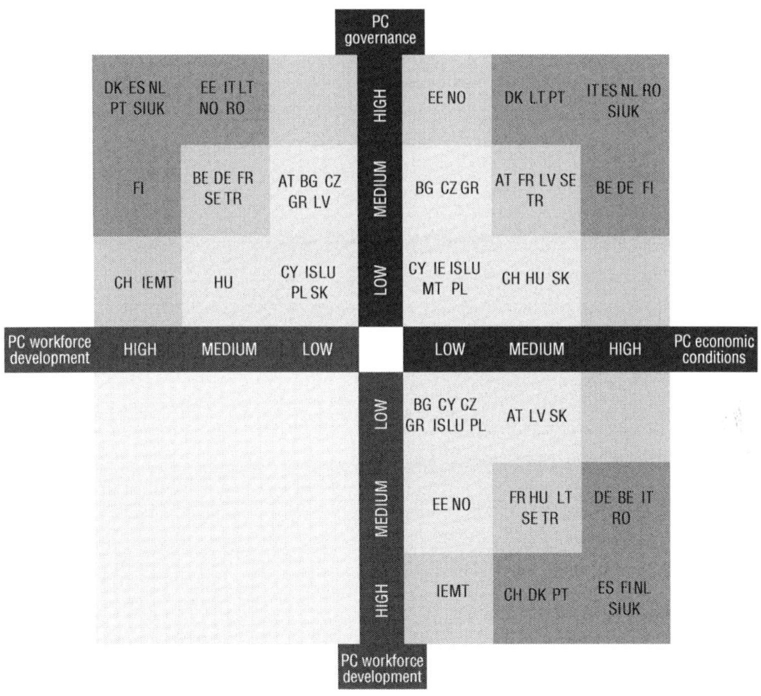

Key: AT – Austria; BE – Belgium; BG – Bulgaria; CH – Switzerland; CY – Cyprus; CZ – Czech Rep.; DE – Germany; DK – Denmark; EE – Estonia; ES – Spain; FI – Finland; FR – France; GR – Greece; HU – Hungary; IE – Ireland; IS – Iceland; IT – Italy; LT – Lithuania; LU – Luxembourg; LV – Latvia; MT – Malta; NL – Netherlands; NO – Norway; PL – Poland; PT – Portugal; RO – Romania; SE – Sweden; SI – Slovenia; SK – Slovakia; TR – Turkey; UK – United Kingdom.

2.5 Good practices and challenges for structuring primary care

In addition to data relevant to the indicators, information was gathered on current priorities and challenges related to structural aspects of primary care. Main points from these reports will be discussed here. The full country reports are in Volume 2.

National strategies and plans

In many countries some explicit and public strategy or more detailed plan is available to guide the development of primary care and against which progress can be assessed. Indeed, the endorsement and effectiveness of such documents are influenced by the political will of administrations and they may be reviewed, changed or completely reformulated as political or economic conditions change.

However, guiding documents on primary care can be an important basis and reference for health service provision to the population. National strategies can be the basis for a comprehensive primary-care based health system. In Spain, for instance, this has been the case during a process of regionalization of its governance and in France a start has been made on developing team-based primary care.

Still there are countries where an explicit plan for the development of primary care, including more comprehensive service provision and better care coordination, is absent. Strong primary care does not develop spontaneously but requires a deliberate explicit policy specifying the division of roles between levels of care, the curative and preventive services provided at the primary care level, the coordination function in the health care system and incentives for providers. Current evidence has shown that health care systems based on a well-developed primary care system perform better in terms of population health and cost-containment. In the absence of explicit policies and regulation on primary care such advantages may be missed.

Inter-professional collaboration

Maintaining the responsiveness of health care systems is a continuing challenge for decision-makers and health professionals. For instance, the ageing of the European population and the increased prevalence of noncommunicable diseases require new ways to cope with changing health needs. Chronic conditions and multi-morbidity can be treated more effectively by different closely collaborating health care workers among whom tasks may be reshuffled. In prevention and anticipatory medicine an integrated primary care level has a major role to play, preferably in relation to community and occupational services. It will be a challenge to realize this, especially in the many countries where the heart of primary care consists of GPs working in solo practice.

Furthermore, professional education should prepare workers for new skills, new skill-mixes and teamwork. Continuing education should also be tuned to changing demands for care and the development of new tasks. Finally, it will be the role of regulation and funding of primary care to create the right incentives to make this work.

Countries that have a better professional infrastructure or a stronger academic tradition in primary care are more often ahead of others in this development. If a vision on the future role of primary care has been developed and formulated countries can learn from each other how to go in this direction.

Education and training

In recent years significant progress has been made in preparing physicians for working in primary care. Mandatory periods of postgraduate training, varying from three to five years, both in universities and in primary care practice, have upgraded the primary care workforce in various countries, although there is much still to be improved. The extent of the training and subjects studied vary considerably, and in a number of countries the domain of general practice is still limited (for instance because GPs are not trained to provide care for children). In some countries postgraduate training for GPs is very limited.

Regarding the professional development of other primary care professions, such as home care nurses and community nurses, the situation is less positive. For these professions the opportunities for obtaining advanced education are limited, mainly to countries in western Europe with well-developed systems of primary care. An integrated and comprehensive primary care service requires investment in people as well as in systems.

Strategies to promote performance

Approaches to encourage better performance in primary care vary across the countries and are related both to the culture and the structure of the health care system. As, in most countries, GPs have a key role in reforms to achieve more efficiency and create more responsive services, performance-related incentives are mostly directed to general practice. Countries may use the force of law without much measurement of actual performance, or they may try incentives, such as pay-for-performance, to make health care workers develop prioritized services and, at the same time, monitor innovative approaches.

2.6 Conclusion

This chapter has depicted aspects of primary care across European countries, in terms of the structure and organization of the primary level of care, including its supporting structures of policy-making, financing, education and workforce.

- Governance for primary care was relatively well developed and differences between countries were modest, but relatively little policy was devoted to multidisciplinary collaboration.

- Concerning the economic conditions, it appeared that expenditures for primary care vary strongly (as far as these could be identified at all). Furthermore, GPs usually earn (much) less than medical specialists. For the rest, differences on economic conditions were small.

- On workforce development differences were larger. Important here were differences between countries in the position of nurses and medical specialists in primary care.

- Taking all dimensions on primary care structure together, a relatively consistent pattern appears: countries ranking high on one dimension are likely to be high on others as well.

References

Frederickson HG (2005). *Whatever happened to public administration? Governance, governance everywhere. The Oxford Handbook of Public Management.* New York, Oxford University Press.

Keohane R (2002). International organizations and garbage can theory. *Journal of Public Administration Research and Theory*, 12:155–159.

Chapter 3

The delivery of primary care services

Andrew Wilson, Adam Windak, Marek Oleszczyk,
Stefan Wilm, Toralf Hasvold, Dionne Kringos

This chapter will be devoted to the dimensions which have been grouped in the framework as "process" and that focus on essential features of service delivery in primary care. In addition to the breadth of services delivered, a comparative overview will be provided of variation in access to services, and continuity and coordination of care. In addition to the volume and type of primary care services, accessibility is determined by the remoteness of services and the practice organization (e.g. appointment system, after-hours care arrangements, home visits). Financial barriers, such as co-payments, determine the financial accessibility of primary care. The extent to which access to primary care services is provided on the basis of health needs, without systematic differences on the basis of individual or social characteristics, indicates the level of equality in access that is achieved. Continuity of care comprises relationship and management continuity. The coordination function reflects the ability of primary care providers to coordinate use of services within primary care and in other levels of health care. It is determined by the presence of a gatekeeping system, practice structure and teamwork, diversification and substitution of primary care providers, and integration and collaboration of primary care with secondary care and the public health sector. This chapter will conclude with a mapping exercise of the breadth of services delivered, accessibility, continuity and coordination of care in countries across Europe, showing also the interrelations across dimensions.

3.1 Access to primary care

An essential feature of primary care is providing access to services for all who need them, irrespective of personal characteristics, socioeconomic status or health status. Accessibility to primary care services is determined by several factors. The volume and types of services should be in good proportion relative to the needs of the population. The remoteness of services in terms of travel distance for patients determines the geographic accessibility of primary care. At practice level, resources should be organized in such a way as to accommodate access (e.g. appointment system, after-hours care arrangements, home visits). Any financial barriers that patients may experience in receiving primary care services, such as co-payments and cost-sharing arrangements, determine the affordability, and thus the financial accessibility of primary care. The extent to which access to primary care services is provided on the basis of health needs, without systematic differences on the basis of individual or social characteristics, indicates the level of equity in access that is achieved. The next section will discuss these features of access to primary care in each of the countries analysed (see Appendix I for a complete overview of all access to primary care features and indicators).

Table 3.1 provides an overview of results of the accessibility of primary care by country.

Provision and distribution of primary care services

A necessary pre-condition for access to primary care is an adequate supply of practitioners, both per head of population nationally, and in their distribution within the country, to ensure there is a match between need for care and its availability. This has long been recognized as a challenge for all health systems (Hart, 1971).

International comparisons of the number of GPs per head of population need to be interpreted cautiously as there is variation in the extent to which primary care is also provided by other medical and nursing disciplines. However, in all countries, the main provider of primary care is the GP. The density of GPs (per 100 000 population), ranges more than sevenfold between European countries.

There are also differences in the distribution of GPs within countries. The largest interregional differences exist in Switzerland, Sweden, Belgium, Bulgaria and the United Kingdom. Least interregional inequality in availability of GPs exists in Portugal, Germany, Slovakia, Hungary and Denmark. There is a lack of quantitative data on urban–rural differences in supply, but several countries have particular difficulties in providing general practice services to rural and deprived urban areas.

In all countries except Austria, Iceland and Spain, shortages of GPs exist according to national norms, either in some regions, or nationwide, as in Cyprus, Finland, Malta, Slovenia, Sweden and Turkey. In Spain, steps have been taken to ensure equitable provision, based on age, rural area and disease prevalence. Norms on the distribution of GPs are absent in Ireland and Luxembourg. Several countries reported concerns that the supply of GPs would become more difficult in the near future because of the ageing workforce; for example in Luxembourg a third of GPs will reach the retirement age in the next 10 years.

Table 3.1

Accessibility of primary care services, overview of selection of results by country

Country	Nr. of GPs per 100 000 population [Year]	Difference between region with highest & lowest density of GPs [Year] (per 100 000 population)	Shortages of GPs according to usual norms	Obligatory minimum opening hours of GP/PC practices	Average nr. of home visits/week by GPs [Year]	Use of telephone consultations in PC practices	Use of e-mail consultations in PC practices	Appointment system use for patient contacts in PC practices	Most frequently used modes of after-hours PC provision [1]	Patient payments for a visit to a GP	Patient payments for prescription medication	Patient payments for a referred specialist visit	Patient payments for a home visit by GP	% patient satisfaction with PC prices & access [Year]
Austria	153.3[07]	17.0[08]	No	Yes	15-	Usually	Seldom / never	Seldom / never	ER; PC cooperatives	No	Some	No	No	Price: 92[07] Access: 94[07]
Belgium	115.0[08]	66.4[08]	Yes some regions	No	37[05]	(Almost) always	Seldom / never	Usually	Practice-based services; ER	Some	Some	Some	Some	Price: 86[07] Access: 97[07]
Bulgaria	66.8[06]	50.0-	Yes some regions	Yes	8-	Usually	Seldom / never	Occasionally	Practice-based services; PC cooperatives; Deputizing services	Some	Some	Some	Some	Price: 84[07] Access: 82[07]
Cyprus	37.4[00]	–	Yes, severely nationwide	Yes	0[10]	Seldom / never	Seldom / never	Occasionally	ER	No	No	No	Full amount	Price: 61[07] Access: 95[07]
Czech Republic	71.0[07]	–	Yes some regions	Yes	5 (–)	Usually	Seldom / never	Occasionally	After-hours PC centres	Some	Some	Some	Some	Price: 95[07] Access: 89[07]
Denmark	74.4[06]	3.0-	Yes some regions	Yes	2.2[09]	(Almost) always	(Almost) always	(Almost) always	PC cooperatives; ER	No	Some	No	No	Price: 99[07] Access: 82
Estonia	62.4[08]	34.0[08]	Yes some regions	Yes	2.2-	Occasionally	Seldom / never	Usually	ER	No	Some	Some	Some	Price: 94[07] Access: 89
Finland	40.6[03]	19.0-	Yes, modestly nationwide	No	–	(Almost) always	Seldom / never	(Almost) always	Practice-based services; PC cooperatives; Deputizing services; ER	Some	Some	Some	Some	Price: 83[07] Access: 92[07]

Country	Nr. of GPs per 100 000 population [Year]	Difference between region with highest & lowest density of GPs [Year] (per 100 000 population)	Shortages of GPs according to usual norms	Obligatory minimum opening hours of GP/PC practices	Average nr. of home visits/ week by GPs [Year]	Use of telephone consultations in PC practices	Use of e-mail consultations in PC practices	Appointment system use for patient contacts in PC practices	Most frequently used modes of after-hours PC provision [1]	Patient payments for a visit to a GP	Patient payments for prescription medication	Patient payments for a referred specialist visit	Patient payments for a home visit by GP	% patient satisfaction with PC prices & access [Year]
France	86.7 [08]	39.5 [07]	Yes some regions	No	13 [08]	(Almost) always	Seldom / never	Usually	Practice-based services; PC cooperatives; ER	Full amount	Some	Full amount	Full amount	Price: 92 [07] Access: 93 [07]
Germany	99.2 [06]	12.4 [08]	Yes some regions	No	25 [02]	(Almost) always	Seldom / never	Occasionally	ER; After-hours PC centres	Some	Some	No	Some	Price: 90 [07] Access: 94 [07]
Greece	35.5 [05]	–	Yes some regions	Yes	–	Occasionally	Seldom / never	Occasionally	After-hours PC centres	No	Some	Some	Some	Price: 57 [07] Access: 78 [07]
Hungary	65.2 [06]	7.7-	Yes some regions	Yes	6.4-	(Almost) always	Seldom / never	Occasionally	Deputizing services	No	Some	No	No	Price: 95 [07] Access: 88 [07]
Iceland	60.0-	–	No	Yes	1-	(Almost) always	Occasionally	(Almost) always	PC cooperatives	Some	Some	Some	Some	Price: – Access: –
Ireland	69.9 [06]	–	No norms	No	–	Usually	Occasionally	(Almost) always	PC cooperatives; After-hours PC centres	Full amount	Full amount	Some	Full amount	Price: 67 [07] Access: 92 [07]
Italy	79.4 [07]	36.7 [07]	Yes some regions	Yes	–	Usually	Occasionally	Occasionally	Practice-based services; PC cooperatives; After-hours PC centres; ER	No	Some	No	Some	Price: 84 [07] Access: 83 [07]
Latvia	58.0 [08]	–	Yes some regions	Yes	4 [09]	(Almost) always	Seldom / never	(Almost) always	ER	Some	Some	Some	Full amount	Price: 95 [07] Access: 73
Lithuania	52.6 [06]	20.0-	Yes some regions	Yes	10 [08]	Occasionally	Occasionally	Usually	ER	No	Some	No	No	Price: 90 [07] Access: 80 [07]
Luxembourg	80.0 [08]	–	No norms	No	10-	Seldom / never	Seldom / never	Usually	ER; After-hours PC centres	Some	Some	Some	Some	Price: 96 [07] Access: 89 [07]

	Malta	Netherlands	Norway	Poland	Portugal	Romania	Slovakia	Slovenia	Spain	Sweden
% patient satisfaction with PC prices & access [Year]	Price: 91'07 Access: 96'07	Price: 91'07 Access: 92'07	Price: – Access: –	Price: 92'07 Access: 90'07	Price: 63'07 Access: 67'07	Price: 76'07 Access: 77'07	Price: 86'07 Access: 83'07	Price: – Access: 86'07	Price: 93'07 Access: 94'07	Price: 96'07 Access: 63'07
Patient payments for a home visit by GP	–	No	Some	No	Some	No	No	No	No	Some
Patient payments for a referred specialist visit	–	Some	Some	No	Some	No	No	No	No	Some
Patient payments for prescription medication	Some	Some	Some	Some	No	No	Some	No	Some	Some
Patient payments for a visit to a GP	Some	No	Some	No	Some	No	No	No	No	Some
Most frequently used modes of after-hours PC provision [1]	–	PC cooperatives	PC cooperatives; After-hours PC centres	Deputizing services; After-hours PC centres	Practice-based services	Deputizing services; ER	After-hours PC centres	PC cooperatives	Practice-based services	PC cooperatives; After-hours PC centres
Appointment system use for patient contacts in PC practices	–	(Almost) always	–	Usually	(Almost) always	Occasionally	Occasionally	(Almost) always	(Almost) always	Usually
Use of e-mail consultations in PC practices	Seldom/never	Seldom/never	Occasionally	Seldom/never	Occasionally	Seldom/never	Seldom/never	Occasionally	Occasionally	Seldom/never
Use of telephone consultations in PC practices	(Almost) always	Usually	(Almost) always	Occasionally	(Almost) always	Occasionally	Seldom/never	Usually	Usually	(Almost) always
Average nr. of home visits/week by GPs [Year]	28'01	9'08	0.4'07	–	0.4'06	5-	9-	3-	–	2'10
Obligatory minimum opening hours of GP/PC practices	Yes	Yes	Yes	Yes	Yes	Yes	No	–	Yes	No
Shortages of GPs according to usual norms	Yes, modestly nationwide	Yes some regions	Yes some regions	No shortage	Yes some regions	Yes some regions	Yes some regions	Yes, severely nationwide	No	Yes, modestly nationwide
Difference between region with highest & lowest density of GPs [Year] (per 100 000 population)	–	16.7'08	36.0'07	24.3'09	13.2'99	–	7.3'07	25.5'07	–	80.0'09
Nr. of GPs per 100 000 population [Year]	77.7'07	47.0'07	47.1'06	20.8'09	62.7'07	80.9'06	50.5'07	46.0'08	84.0'07	60.2'06

Country	Nr. of GPs per 100 000 population [Year]	Difference between region with highest & lowest density of GPs [Year] (per 100 000 population)	Shortages of GPs according to usual norms	Obligatory minimum opening hours of GP/PC practices	Average nr. of home visits/week by GPs [Year]	Use of telephone consultations in PC practices	Use of e-mail consultations in PC practices	Appointment system use for patient contacts in PC practices	Most frequently used modes of after-hours PC provision [1]	Patient payments for a visit to a GP	Patient payments for prescription medication	Patient payments for a referred specialist visit	Patient payments for a home visit by GP	% patient satisfaction with PC prices & access [Year]
Switzerland	103.0 [08]	539.0 [09]	Yes some regions	No	–	(Almost) always	Seldom / never	Usually	After-hours PC centres; ER; Practice-based services	Some	Some	Some	Some	Price: 95 [07] Access: –
Turkey	52.5 [08]	34.0 [08]	Yes, severely nationwide	Yes	1 [07]	Occasionally	Seldom / never	Seldom / never	Practice-based services	No	Some	No	No	Price: 71 [07] Access: 60 [07]
United Kingdom	72.0 [07]	42.9 [05] (ENG)	Yes some regions	Yes	6 [06]	(Almost) always	Occasionally	(Almost) always	After-hours PC centres; Deputizing services	No	Some	No	No	Price: 96 [07] Access: 86 [07]

1 Practice-based services = GPs within one practice or organized in a group of practices look after their patients on out-of-hours schedules; PC cooperatives = GPs in a region from several groups, supported by additional personnel, provide after-hours PC mostly in non-profit, large-scale organizations, which include telephone triage and advice, office for face-to-face contact, and house calls; Deputizing services (outsourcing) = companies employing doctors take over the provision of after-hours care; ER = Hospital emergency departments provide PC by taking care of health problems after office hours; After-hours PC centres = These are (walk-in) centres for face-to-face contact with a GP or nurse.

Availability of primary care services

In addition to the provision of services, access relies on primary care services being available at times that suit the population, and for emergencies outside normal working hours. Primary care centres are obliged to have a minimum number of opening hours in all countries except Belgium, Finland, France, Germany, Ireland, Luxembourg, Slovakia, Sweden and Switzerland. However, there is marked variation in the minimum number of hours required per week, from 20 in Austria to 52.5 in the United Kingdom. In several countries (e.g. Norway), minimum opening hours are determined locally, and in others (e.g. Italy) they vary according to the number of registered patients.

There is a diversity of models for out-of-hours care (Huibers et al., 2009). Several countries report multiple systems, but the most common models are non-practice-based provision (including cooperatives, primary care centres and deputizing services) followed by practice-based services (based around one or more practices). Out-of-hours care supplied by emergency departments has been recognized as having weaknesses in terms of continuity, cost, coordination and accessibility (Huibers et al., 2009). The extent to which these departments contribute to out-of-hours care varies across Europe, but it is notable that in Cyprus, Estonia, Latvia and Lithuania emergency departments have the sole responsibility for after-hours primary care service delivery.

Types of contact

Appointment systems can facilitate access or make access more difficult, depending on their flexibility and responsiveness (Pascoe, Neal & Allgar, 2004). The extent to which appointment systems are used varies between countries; they are not frequently used in Austria, Bulgaria, Cyprus, the Czech Republic, Germany, Greece, Hungary, Italy, Romania, Slovakia and Turkey.

The extent of home visiting differs largely across Europe. The five countries with the highest average number of home visits per week by GPs are Belgium (37), Malta (28), Germany (25), Austria (15) and France (13); and the lowest are Portugal and Norway (both less than 1), Iceland and Turkey (both 1), and Cyprus, where no home visits are made. Although some of this variation is because of cultural or demographic reasons, it is likely that access to usual primary care is a problem for housebound and severely ill patients in countries such as Cyprus, where GPs do not offer any visits at all, and in countries with very low rates of home visits.

Access to primary care can be enhanced by the provision of a range of options beyond the traditional face-to-face consultation. Telephone consultations are usually offered, except in Cyprus, Estonia, Greece, Lithuania, Luxembourg,

Poland, Romania, Slovakia and Turkey. E-mail consultations are frequently offered only in Denmark, and occasionally in Iceland, Ireland, Italy, Lithuania, Norway, Portugal, Slovenia, Spain and the United Kingdom.

In 2007, patient satisfaction with ease in reaching and gaining access to GPs was lowest in Turkey, Sweden, Portugal (60–69%), Latvia, Romania, Greece (70–79%), Lithuania, Bulgaria, Denmark, Italy and Slovakia (80–85%), with rates of 90% or higher in Austria, Belgium, Cyprus, Finland, Germany, Ireland, Malta, the Netherlands, Poland and Spain.

Financial barriers to access

In addition to geographical and organizational access, it is essential that financial barriers do not impede access to primary care services. In the majority of countries (16) there is no payment for a visit to a GP, while in 15 there are co-payments. Payment for a home visit by a GP is more common; there is no charge in only 12 countries, with co-payments in 14 and full payments in four (Cyprus, France, Ireland and Latvia). Payments for prescribed drugs are a lot more common; there is no charge in only four countries (Cyprus, Portugal, Romania and Slovenia).

Most countries apply one or more of the following criteria for exemptions for co-payments on primary care services: disadvantaged groups (income, employment status, legal status), pregnant women, children, young people in full-time education, blood donors, pensioners, war veterans, groups of patients with specific diseases (often chronic conditions), being registered in a health centre (only in Belgium) or preventive visits. Some countries have a ceiling for co-payments specifically for primary care services, medicines, or all medical care.

The level of co-payments often depends on the insurance status of patients, and the employment status of primary care providers. The highest (formal) payments in the public system exist in Ireland, where patients without a medical card (over 60% of the population) pay €45–60 for each general practice visit, with no reimbursement. In Switzerland no exemptions are made for primary care services, as patients have a deductible of CHF 300–2500 (€225–1875), depending on the insurance contract, and pay 10% of the physician fee up to CHF 700 (€525) a year after this limit is reached. As a result, 66% of the primary care physicians' costs are paid out of pocket by patients in Switzerland. Patients who cannot afford health care services depend on social services. In a decentralized country like Sweden, medical care fees differ across the countries. For example, co-payments for visits to GPs range from SEK 150–300 (€14.69–29.38). Higher fees apply for out-of-hours consultations. In France, there is a general tendency for increasing out-of-pocket payments, even with a complementary insurance, and especially for primary care. In Hungary and Romania physicians use a tipping system, expecting an extra (unofficial) out-of-pocket payment from their patients. This means that the official system can be very different from the unofficial system. Out-of pocket payments in the private sector can also be very high across Europe. For example, when a patient insured via an SHI fund in Greece visits a private (not contracted) physician he or she has to pay market prices and will receive a fixed reimbursement of €20, which is often at least €50 lower than the price paid.

The following countries had the lowest levels of patient satisfaction with the costs of general practice care in 2007: Greece (57%), Cyprus (61%), Portugal (63%), Ireland (67%), Turkey (71%), Romania (76%), Finland (83%), Italy (84%) and Belgium (86%).

Overall accessibility of primary care

Fig. 3.1 shows the total access to primary care score by country, considering the performance of each country on all access indicators (see Appendix II for the applied scoring system).

Many countries had difficulties reporting inequalities in geographical density of GPs. Of the 21 countries with available data, only six had relatively low inequalities in geographical availability of primary care services, and many reported shortages in supply. Another important aspect requiring improvement is the accommodation of access through home visits, e-mail consultations or use of appointment systems, which vary greatly across Europe. The perceived affordability of primary care by patients seemed to be an important aspect limiting access to primary care in several countries.

When considering all features of access to care, Slovenia, Denmark, Spain, the United Kingdom, the Netherlands, Poland, the Czech Republic, Portugal, Hungary and Lithuania have a relatively high accessibility of primary care. Access is relatively low in Ireland, Luxembourg, Turkey, France, Greece, Cyprus, Belgium, Bulgaria, Latvia, Malta and Switzerland. All other countries have a medium level of access to primary care. The difference between the highest and lowest performing countries is relatively high.

Fig. 3.1
Total access to primary care score by country (scale 1 (low) – 3 (high))

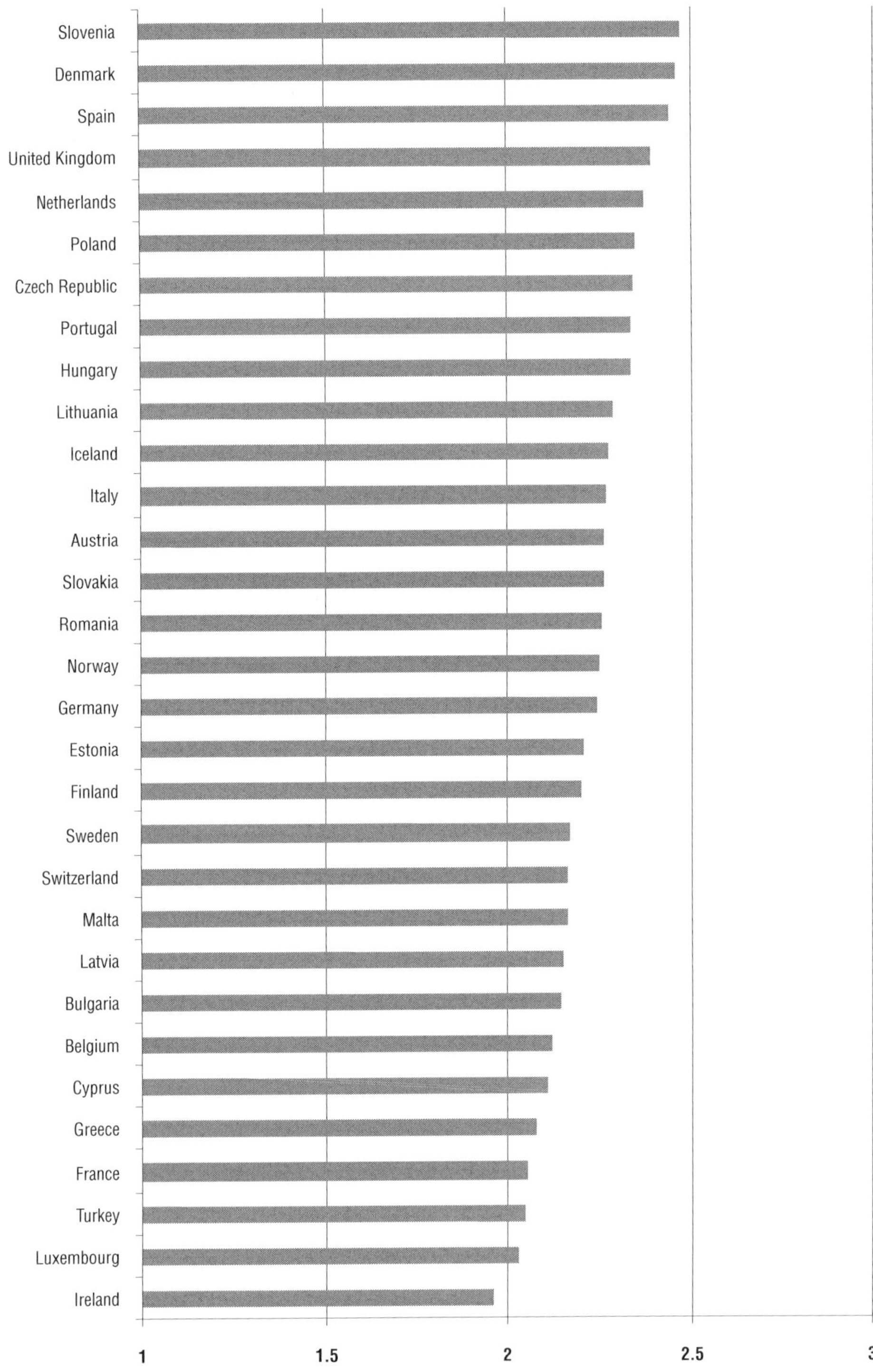

3.2 Continuity of primary care

Continuity of care consists of relationship continuity and management continuity (Hill & Freeman, 2011). Relationship continuity implies that patients benefit from having a long-term relationship with a primary care provider that goes beyond specific episodes of illness or disease. Some definitions also speak of personal or family continuity, where the continuity of care between a single provider or a family is stressed. The quality of the longitudinal relationship between primary care providers and patients, in terms of accommodation of patients' needs and preferences, such as communication and respect for patients, determine relationship continuity. Management continuity involves coordination and teamwork between caregivers and across organizational boundaries. It includes an organized collection of each patient's medical information readily available to any health care provider caring for the patient. This can be reached through medical record-keeping, clinical support and referral systems. The next section will discuss these features of continuity of primary care in each of the countries analysed (see Appendix I for an overview of the Continuity of Care features, indicators and additional information items).

Table 3.2 provides an overview of results of the continuity of primary care by country.

Table 3.2

Continuity of primary care services, overview of selection of results by country

Country	Use of patient list system by GPs	Average population size per GP	% patients reported visiting usual PC provider for common health problems	Availability of computer in GP's office	Purpose of computer in general practice [1]	Use of referral letters by GPs	Incoming clinical info. procedures about after-hours patient contacts	Specialist–GP communication on completed patient care	Patients' freedom to choose a PC centre (PCC) and GP to register	% patients satisfied with: relation with their GP/PC physician	% patients satisfied with: available time during visits to GP/PC physician	% patients satisfied with: trust in their GP/ PC physician	% patients satisfied with: explanation by GP/PC physician on treatment
Austria	No	2000	65	(Almost) always	ADM; MED; REC	Occasionally	Occasionally	Occasionally	PCC: Yes GP: Yes	–	–	–	–
Belgium	No	718	80	Usually	APP; MED; REC; INT; SPE	Usually	Occasionally	Usually	PCC: Yes GP: Yes	85	80	90	85
Bulgaria	Yes	1654	85	(Almost) always	ADM; MED; REC; INT	(Almost) always	Occasionally	Usually	PCC: Yes GP: Yes	80	60	70	70
Cyprus	No	–	–	Usually	ADM; MED; REC	–	–	–	PCC: Yes GP: Yes	90	85	95	90
Czech Republic	Yes	1613	93	(Almost) always	ADM; MED; REC	Usually	Usually	(Almost) always	PCC: Yes GP: Yes	–	–	–	–
Denmark	Yes	1583	–	(Almost) always	APP; ADM; MED; REC; INT; SPE; PHA	(Almost) always	(Almost) always	(Almost) always	PCC: Yes GP: Yes	86	77	–	79
Estonia	Yes	1596	70	(Almost) always	ADM; MED; REC	(Almost) always	(Almost) always	Usually	PCC: Yes GP: Yes	92	–	98	96
Finland	Yes	1900	–	(Almost) always	APP; ADM; MED; REC; INT; SPE; PHA	(Almost) always	Usually	Usually	PCC: No, assigned GP: Yes	90	75	80	80
France	No	800	90	(Almost) always	ADM; MED; REC	(Almost) always	Seldom/ never	Usually	PCC: Yes GP: Yes	–	90	–	91
Germany	No	2000	95	(Almost) always	ADM; MED; REC	(Almost) always	Usually	Usually	PCC: Yes GP: Yes	92	90	92	90
Greece	Yes	–	–	(Almost) always	ADM; MED; REC; INT; SPE; PHA	Seldom / never	Occasionally	–	PCC: No, assigned GP: Yes	90	80	99	97

	Hungary	Iceland	Ireland	Italy	Latvia	Lithuania	Luxembourg	Malta	Netherlands	Norway	Poland	Portugal	Romania
% patients satisfied with: explanation by GP/PC physician on treatment	60	–	72	–	87	60	–	–	70	78	–	–	60
% patients satisfied with: trust in their GP/PC physician	80	–	93	–	72	60	–	–	74	93	–	–	75
% patients satisfied with: available time during visits to GP/PC physician	40	–	–	–	79	50	–	–	26	73	88	–	75
% patients satisfied with: relation with their GP/PC physician	84	–	93	–	93	70	–	–	70	94	86	75	80
Patients' freedom to choose a PC centre (PCC) and GP to register	PCC: Yes GP: Yes	PCC: Yes GP: Yes	PCC: Yes GP: Yes	PCC: Yes GP: Yes	PCC: Yes GP: Yes	PCC: Yes GP: Yes	PCC: Yes GP: Yes	PCC: Yes GP: Yes	PCC: Yes GP: Yes	PCC: Yes GP: Yes	PCC: Yes GP: Yes	PCC: Yes GP: Yes	PCC: Yes GP: Yes
Specialist–GP communication on completed patient care	Usually	Usually	(Almost) always	Usually	Usually	Usually	Usually	Usually	(Almost) always	Usually	Usually	Usually	(Almost) always
Incoming clinical info. procedures about after-hours patient contacts	Occasionally	Usually	Usually	Occasionally	Seldom / never	Occasionally	Seldom / never	Seldom / never	Occasionally	Usually	Occasionally	Occasionally	Occasionally
Use of referral letters by GPs	Usually	Usually	(Almost) always	Seldom / never	(Almost) always	(Almost) always	Usually	–	(Almost) always	(Almost) always	(Almost) always	(Almost) always	(Almost) always
Purpose of computer in general practice [1]	MED; REC	ADM; MED; REC; INT	APP; ADM; MED; REC	APP; MED; REC; INT; SPE	APP; ADM; REC; INT	APP; ADM; REC; INT	ADM; MED; REC	ADM	ADM; MED; REC; PHA	ADM; MED; REC	ADM	APP; MED; REC; INT; SPE	ADM; REC
Availability of computer in GP's office	(Almost) always	(Almost) always	Usually	Usually	Occasionally	Occasionally	Usually	Occasionally	(Almost) always	(Almost) always	(Almost) always	(Almost) always	Usually
% patients reported visiting usual PC provider for common health problems	90	85	–	–	80	80	–	80	71 -	71	85	67	85
Average population size per GP	1530	1550	1680	1094	1585	1550	500 -	2500	2322	1219	1539	1500	2000
Use of patient list system by GPs	Yes	Yes	No	Yes	Yes	Yes	No	No	Yes	Yes	Yes	Yes	Yes

Country	% patients satisfied with: explanation by GP/PC physician on treatment	% patients satisfied with: trust in their GP/PC physician	% patients satisfied with: available time during visits to GP/PC physician	% patients satisfied with: relation with their GP/PC physician	Patients' freedom to choose a PC centre (PCC) and GP to register	Specialist–GP communication on completed patient care	Incoming clinical info. procedures about after-hours patient contacts	Use of referral letters by GPs	Purpose of computer in general practice[1]	Availability of computer in GP's office	% patients reported visiting usual PC provider for common health problems	Average population size per GP	Use of patient list system by GPs
Slovakia	87	90	85	84	PCC: Yes GP: Yes	(Almost) always	Usually	(Almost) always	ADM; MED; REC	(Almost) always	98	2163	Yes
Slovenia	49	–	92	81	PCC: Yes GP: No, assigned	Usually	Occasionally	(Almost) always	ADM; REC	Usually	93	1789	Yes
Spain	90	92	88	95	PCC: Yes GP: Yes	–	Usually	(Almost) always	ADM; MED; REC; SPE; PHA	(Almost) always	72	1500	Yes
Sweden	–	–	–	55	PCC: No, assigned GP: Yes	(Almost) always	Occasionally	(Almost) always	ADM; MED; REC; INT; PHA	Usually	–	–	No
Switzerland	–	–	–	–	PCC: Yes GP: Yes	(Almost) always	(Almost) always	Usually	ADM; REC; INT	Usually	88	–	No
Turkey	88	59	86	94	PCC: Yes GP: Yes	Seldom / never	Occasionally	Occasionally	REC; INT	(Almost) always	78	3687	Yes
United Kingdom	79	95	90	85	PCC: Yes GP: Yes	(Almost) always	(Almost) always	(Almost) always	APP; ADM; MED; REC	(Almost) always	77 (ENG)	1745	Yes

1 APP = Booking appointments with patients; ADM = Writing bills/financial administration; MED = Prescription of medicines; REC = Keeping medical records of patients; INT = Searching expert information on the Internet; SPE = Communicating patient information to specialists; PHA = Communicating prescriptions to pharmacists.

Continuity of care over time

Continuity of primary care is facilitated in primary care by GPs having a list of patients for whose medical care they are responsible, either personally or as a group. Such lists of registered patients are the norm in most countries of Europe, and mandatory in all countries except Austria, Belgium, Cyprus, France, Germany, Ireland, Luxembourg, Malta, Sweden and Switzerland. In some of these countries, registration with a GP is compulsory for some patients (e.g. those who are state funded in Ireland) or incentivized (e.g. by a reduction of co-payments in Belgium).

The average population size served by GPs is 1687 patients. GPs have the largest average list size in Turkey (3687), Malta (2500), the Netherlands (2322) and the Slovakia (2163); and the smallest in Luxembourg (500), Belgium (718), France (800), Italy (1094) and Norway (1219).

There is potentially a trade-off between choice and continuity. Patients are free to register with any primary care centre and GP in their locality in all countries except Finland, Greece and Sweden, where patients are assigned to a primary care centre, and Slovenia, where patients are assigned to a GP. Continuity is best achieved by patients visiting their usual primary care provider for their common health problems rather than attending multiple primary care providers or medical specialists. Interpretation of results regarding this aspect is difficult as some national data sets define the usual provider as an individual clinician, whereas in others it is defined as an organization. The extent to which other professionals (e.g. pharmacists and nurses) are used for common health problems also varies between countries. In all 23 counties where data were available, it was found to be "usually the case" that patients consulted the same provider for their common health problems, although this varied from a high of over 90% in the Czech Republic and Slovakia to lows of below 70% in Austria and Portugal.

Management continuity

Management continuity relies on good information systems, both within primary care and between primary and secondary care. GPs' offices in all countries (except Latvia, Lithuania and Malta) are usually equipped with a computer for keeping medical records, financial administration and prescription of medicines. In only a minority of countries computers are also used for researching expert information on the Internet, booking appointments, and for communication with medical specialists or pharmacists. Finland and Denmark have the highest use of computers in general practice. Referral letters are usually used by all GPs in Europe, except in Austria, Greece, Italy and Turkey (no data available for Cyprus and Malta). In most (18) countries it takes more than 24 hours to receive information about out-of-hours contacts for patients.

Relationship continuity

On average 85% of patients in Europe are satisfied with their relationship with their primary care physician and trust their primary care physician. Satisfaction with the patient–primary care physician relationship is lowest in Sweden (55%), Lithuania (70%) and the Netherlands (70%); and patients least trust their primary care physician in Turkey (59%), Lithuania (60%), Bulgaria (70%) and Latvia (72%). On average, only 79% of patients in Europe were satisfied with the explanation given by their primary care providers of problems, procedures and treatments. This is lowest in Slovenia (49%), Hungary (60%), Lithuania (60%) and Romania (60%).

Overall continuity of primary care by country

Fig. 3.2 shows the total score of continuity of primary care by country (see Appendix II for the applied scoring system). Variation between countries appears to be very small. Only Turkey, Malta and Austria have lower scores. The difference between the other countries is negligible.

In countries where GPs have a high patient load, relationship continuity can be improved by limiting the average population size per GP. This would reduce the work load and increase possibilities for building a high-quality relationship with patients. Patient satisfaction with several aspects of their relationship with their GP (e.g. consultation duration) could be improved in many countries.

3.3 Coordination of primary care

Primary care physicians can have an important role in coordinating the health care of their patients, including coordination within primary care, coordination of input from medical specialists, and coordination with public health to address broader public health issues. Lack of coordination of specialist care can lead to unnecessary costs, duplication of services and higher risk of medical errors. The next section will discuss the important features of coordination of primary care in each of the countries analysed (see Appendix I for an overview of the coordination of care features and indicators).

Table 3.3 provides an overview of a selection of results of the coordination of primary care by country.

Fig. 3.2

Total continuity of primary care score by country (scale 1 (low) – 3 (high))

Table 3.3

Coordination of primary care services, overview of selection of results by country

| Country | Referral system | | | Gatekeeping system in place | % single-handed GP practices | % GP group & mixed GP specialist practices | GPs have regular face-to-face meetings with [1,2] | Common use of nurse-led diabetes clinics & n-l. health education in PC [3] | Commonly used form of cooperation between GP/PC medical specialists [4] | GPs regularly ask telephone advice from specialists [1,5] | Use of clinical patient records to identify health policy priorities | Use of community health surveys to improve quality of PC |
	Patients have direct access to [1]	Patients need a referral to access [1]	Patients have direct access if costs are privately paid [1]									
Austria	INT; OPH; ENT; CAR; SUR; PCN; HCN; PHT; MID; OCT; SPCH	–	OB/GYN; PAED; NEU; SPN; DEN	No	95	Group: 5 Mixed: 0	None	DC: No HE: No	None	None	Seldom / never	Incidentally, regionally/ locally
Belgium	OB/GYN; PAED; INT; OPH; ENT; CAR; NEU; SUR; PCN; MID; DEN	–	SPN; HCN; PHT; OCT; SPCH	No	76	Group: 24 Mixed: 0	GP; PCN; NP; HCN; CPH	DC: No HE: No	CL	INT; NEU; DER; GER	Seldom / never	Regularly, nationwide
Bulgaria	DEN	OB/GYN; PAED; INT; OPH; ENT; CAR; NEU; SUR; PHT; OCT; SPCH	PCN; SPN; HCN	Yes	95	Group: 5 Mixed: 0	PCN	DC: No HE: No	None	None	Seldom / never	Incidentally, regionally/ locally
Cyprus	OB/GYN; PAED; INT; OPH; ENT; CAR; NEU; SUR; PCN; SPN; HCN; DEN	PHT; MID; OCT; SPCH	–	No	20	Group: 60 Mixed: 20	PCN; NP; CPHAR	DC: No HE: No	None	INT; SUR; NEU; DER	Seldom / never	Incidentally, regionally/ locally
Czech Republic	OB/GYN; PAED; OPH; CAR; PCN; PHT	SPN; HCN; DEN	INT; ENT; NEU; SUR; OCT; SPCH	No, but incentives	95	Group: 4 Mixed: 1	GP; PCN; NP; HCN; CPH	DC: No HE: No	CL	PAED; INT	Seldom / never	Incidentally, regionally/ locally
Denmark	OPH; ENT; DEN	PCN; SPN; HCN; MID; OCT; SPCH	OB/GYN; PAED; INT; CAR; NEU; SUR; PHT	No, but incentives	36	Group: 64 Mixed: 0	GP; PCN DC: Yes	HE: Yes	CL	None	Incidentally	Incidentally, nationwide

	Estonia	Finland	France	Germany	Greece	Hungary	Iceland	Ireland
Use of community health surveys to improve quality of PC	Regularly, nationwide	Incidentally, regionally/locally	Incidentally, regionally/locally	Incidentally, regionally/locally	Incidentally, regionally/locally	Incidentally, regionally/locally	Incidentally, regionally/locally	Incidentally, regionally/locally
Use of clinical patient records to identify health policy priorities	Routinely	Incidentally	Seldom/never	Seldom/never	Incidentally	Seldom/never	Incidentally	Seldom/never
GPs regularly ask telephone advice from specialists [1,5]	None	None	SUR	None	–	None	None	None
Commonly used form of cooperation between GP/PC medical specialists [4]	CL	CL	CL	None	–	None	None	None
Common use of nurse-led diabetes clinics & n-l. health education in PC [3]	DC: No HE: No	DC: No HE: Yes	DC: No HE: No	DC: No HE: No	DC: – HE: –	DC: No HE: No	DC: – HE: –	DC: No HE: No
GPs have regular face-to-face meetings with [1,2]	GP; PCN	GP; PCN; NP	None	PCN	GP; PCN; NP; MID; PHT; CPH; SW; CMH	GP; PCN; HCN	GP; PCN; NP; MID; SW	GP; PCN; NP; HCN; MID; PHT
% GP group & mixed GP specialist practices	Group: 23 Mixed: 0	Group: 98 Mixed: 1	Group: 54 Mixed: 0	Group: 29 Mixed: 9	Group: 40 Mixed: 20	Group: 4 Mixed: 1	Group: 85 Mixed: 0	Group: 70 Mixed: 0
% single-handed GP practices	77	1	46	62	40	95	15	30
Referral system — Gatekeeping system in place	Yes	No, but incentives	No, but incentives	No	No, but incentives	Yes, partially	No, but incentives	No, but incentives
Patients have direct access if costs are privately paid [1]	–	OB/GYN; PAED; INT; OPH; ENT; CAR; NEU; SUR; PHT	ENT; CAR; NEU; SUR; PHT; SPCH	HCN; PHT; OCT; SPCH	OB/GYN; PAED; INT; OPH; ENT; CAR; NEU; SUR; PCN; SPN	–	OB/GYN; PAED; INT; OPH; ENT; CAR; NEU; SUR	OB/GYN; PAED; INT; OPH; ENT; CAR; NEU; SUR; DEN
Patients need a referral to access [1]	PAED; INT; ENT; CAR; NEU; SUR; SPN; HCN; PHT; SPCH	OCT; SPCH; MID; DEN	INT; OCT	SPN	HCN; PHT; MID; OCT; SPCH; DEN	INT; CAR; NEU; SPN; HCN; PHT; OCT; SPCH	–	SPN
Patients have direct access to [1]	OB/GYN; OPH; PCN; MID; OCT	PCN; SPN; HCN; MID; DEN	OB/GYN; PAED; OPH; MID; DEN	OB/GYN; PAED; INT; OPH; ENT; CAR; NEU; SUR; PCN; MID; DEN	–	OB/GYN; PAED; OPH; ENT; SUR; PCN; MID; DEN	PCN; SPN; HCN; PHT; MID; OCT; SPCH; DEN	PCN; HCN; PHT; MID; OCT; SPCH
Country	Estonia	Finland	France	Germany	Greece	Hungary	Iceland	Ireland

Country	Patients have direct access to [1]	Patients need a referral to access [1]	Patients have direct access if costs are privately paid [1]	Gatekeeping system in place	% single-handed GP practices	% GP group & mixed GP specialist practices	GPs have regular face-to-face meetings with [1,2]	Common use of nurse-led diabetes clinics & n-l. health education in PC [3]	Commonly used form of cooperation between GP/PC medical specialists [4]	GPs regularly ask telephone advice from specialists [1,5]	Use of clinical patient records to identify health policy priorities	Use of community health surveys to improve quality of PC
Italy	PAED; PCN; MID	INT; OPH; ENT; CAR; NEU; SUR; SPN; HCN; OCT; SPCH	OB/GYN; PHT; DEN	Yes	78	Group: 22 Mixed: 0	GP; PCN; NP; HCN; SW; CMH	DC: No HE: No	CL	INT; GER	Incidentally	Incidentally, regionally/locally
Latvia	OB/GYN; PAED; OPH; PCN; MID	INT; ENT; CAR; NEU; SUR; SPN; HCN; PHT; OCT; SPCH	DEN	Yes, partially	92	Group: 0 Mixed: 8	GP; PCN; NP	DC: No HE: No	CL	NEU	Seldom / never	Incidentally, nationwide
Lithuania	DEN	OB/GYN; PAED; INT; OPH; ENT; CAR; NEU; SUR; PCN; SPN; HCN; PHT; MID; OCT; SPCH	–	Yes	5	Group: 15 Mixed: 80	GP; PCN; NP; HCN	DC: No HE: Yes	RSP	PAED; INT; GYN; SUR; NEU; DER; GER	Routinely	Incidentally, nationwide
Luxembourg	OB/GYN; PAED; INT; OPH; ENT; CAR; NEU; SUR; DEN	PCN; SPN; PHT; MID; OCT; SPCH	HCN	No	70	Group: 30 Mixed: 0	HCN; PHT; SW	DC: No HE: No	CL	INT; SUR; NEU	Seldom / never	None
Malta	PCN; MID; DEN	SPN; HCN; PHT	OB/GYN; PAED; INT; OPH; ENT; CAR; NEU; SUR; OCT; SPCH	No, but incentives	70	Group: 10 Mixed: 20	None	DC: No HE: Yes	CL	None	Seldom / never	Incidentally, regionally/locally
Netherlands	PCN; SPN; HCN; PHT; MID; OCT; DEN	OB/GYN; PAED; INT; OPH; ENT; CAR; NEU; SUR; SPCH	–	Yes	42	Group: 58 Mixed: 0	GP; PCN; NP; HCN; PHT; CPH; SW; CMH	DC: Yes HE: Yes	CL	PAED; INT; GYN; SUR; NEU; DER; GER	Routinely	Regularly, nationwide
Norway	PCN; SPN; HCN; MID; OCT; DEN	OB/GYN; PAED; INT; OPH; ENT; CAR; NEU; SUR; PHT; SPCH	–	Yes	–	Group: – Mixed: –	None	DC: No HE: No	None	PAED; INT; GYN; SUR; NEU; DER; GER	Incidentally	Incidentally, regionally/locally

Note: the three columns "Patients have direct access to [1]", "Patients need a referral to access [1]" and "Patients have direct access if costs are privately paid [1]" fall under the heading *Referral system*.

	Poland	Portugal	Romania	Slovakia	Slovenia	Spain	Sweden	Switzerland
Use of community health surveys to improve quality of PC	Incidentally, nationwide	Regularly, regionally/locally	Regularly, nationwide	Incidentally, regionally/locally	–	Regularly, nationwide	Regularly, nationwide	Regularly, nationwide
Use of clinical patient records to identify health policy priorities	Seldom / never	Routinely	Routinely	Seldom / never	Routinely	Routinely	Routinely	Seldom / never
GPs regularly ask telephone advice from specialists [1,5]	None	None	–	None	None	PAED; GYN	PAED; INT; GYN; SUR; DER; GER	INT; SUR; NEU; DER
Commonly used form of cooperation between GP/PC medical specialists [4]	CL	None	None	None	CL	RSP	RSP; JC; CL	CL
Common use of nurse-led diabetes clinics & n-l. health education in PC [3]	DC: No HE: Yes	DC: No HE: Yes	DC: No HE: Yes	DC: No HE: No	DC: No HE: Yes	DC: No HE: Yes	DC: Yes HE: Yes	DC: No HE: No
GPs have regular face-to-face meetings with [1,2]	GP; PCN; NP; MID	GP; PCN	GP; PCN	None	GP; PCN; NP; HCN; MID; PHT	GP; PCN	GP; PCN; NP; HCN; MID; PHT; SW; CMH	GP; HCN
% GP group & mixed GP specialist practices	Group: 94 Mixed: 0	Group: 100 Mixed: 0	Group: 26 Mixed: 7	Group: 0 Mixed: 0	Group: 60 Mixed: 20	Group: 97 Mixed: 3	Group: 97 Mixed: 0	Group: 37 Mixed: 0
% single-handed GP practices	6	0	67	100	20	0	3	63
Gatekeeping system in place	No, but incentives	Yes	Yes	No, but incentives	Yes	Yes	Yes, partially	No
Referral system — Patients have direct access if costs are privately paid [1]	PAED; INT; ENT; CAR; NEU; SUR; PHT; OCT; SPCH	–	PCN	INT; ENT; CAR; NEU; SUR; HCN; PHT; OCT; SPCH	–	–	–	PHT; DEN
Referral system — Patients need a referral to access [1]	SPN; HCN	OB/GYN; PAED; INT; OPH; CAR; NEU; SUR; SPN; HCN; PHT; MID; OCT; SPCH; DEN	OB/GYN; INT; OPH; ENT; CAR; NEU; SUR	–	INT; OPH; ENT; CAR; NEU; SUR; PHT; OCT; SPCH	INT; OPH; ENT; CAR; NEU; SUR; SPN; PHT; OCT; SPCH	INT; OPH; ENT; CAR; NEU; SUR	SPN; HCN
Referral system — Patients have direct access to [1]	OB/GYN; OPH; PCN; MID; DEN	PCN	–	OB/GYN; PAED; OPH; DEN	OB/GYN; PAED; PCN; HCN; DEN	OB/GYN; PAED; PCN; HCN; MID; DEN	OB/GYN; PAED; PCN; SPN; HCN; PHT; MID; OCT; SPCH; DEN	OB/GYN; PAED; INT; OPH; ENT; CAR; NEU; SUR; PCN; MID; OCT; SPCH

Country	Patients have direct access to[1]	Patients need a referral to access[1]	Patients have direct access if costs are privately paid[1]	Gatekeeping system in place	% single-handed GP practices	% GP group & mixed GP specialist practices	GPs have regular face-to-face meetings with[1,2]	Common use of nurse-led diabetes clinics & n-l. health education in PC[3]	Commonly used form of cooperation between GP/PC medical specialists[4]	GPs regularly ask telephone advice from specialists[1,5]	Use of clinical patient records to identify health policy priorities	Use of community health surveys to improve quality of PC
		Referral system										
Turkey	OB/GYN; PAED; INT; OPH; ENT; CAR; NEU; SUR; PCN; SPN; HCN; PHT; MID; OCT; SPCH; DEN	–	–	No	4	Group: 96 Mixed: 0	GP; PCN	DC: Yes HE: Yes	None	None	Routinely	Incidentally, regionally/ locally
United Kingdom	PCN; MID; DEN	OB/GYN; PAED; INT; OPH; ENT; CAR; NEU; SUR; SPN; HCN; PHT; OCT; SPCH	–	Yes	21	Group: 78 Mixed: 1	GP; PCN; NP; HCN; MID	DC: Yes HE: No	CL	None	Routinely	Regularly, nationwide

1 GP/FP = GP/Family Physician; OB/GYN = Obstetrician/Gynaecologist; PAED = Paediatrician; INT = Specialist of Internal medicine; OPH = Ophthalmologist; ENT = Ear Nose Throat Specialist; CAR = Cardiologist; NEU = Neurologist; SUR = Surgeon; PCN = Primary care/General practice nurse; SPN = Specialized nurse; HCN = Home care nurse; PHT = Physiotherapist (ambulatory); MID = Midwife (ambulatory); OCT = Occupational therapist; SPCH = Speech therapist; DEN = Dentist.
2 NP = Nurse practitioner; CPH = Community pharmacist; SW = Social worker; CMH = Community mental health worker.
3 DC = Nurse-led diabetes clinics; HE = Nurse-led health education. 4 RSP = Medical specialists visiting a PC practice to provide specialist care normally provided in hospital (replaced specialist care); JC = Medical specialist visiting a PC practice to provide joint care with a GP (joint consultation); CL = Clinical lessons by a medical specialist for GPs. 5 DER = Dermatologist; GER = Geriatrist.

Gatekeeping

One method of achieving coordinated care is for access to a specialist to be available only by referral from the patient's GP, the so-called "gatekeeper" function. Between a full gatekeeping role for GPs and no gatekeeping, two other models can be distinguished. So the following four variants can be identified among countries in Europe:

1. No gatekeeping system in place. Patients, with a few possible exceptions, have direct access to most physicians (Austria, Belgium, Cyprus, Germany, Luxembourg, Switzerland, Turkey);

2. No formal gatekeeping system in place, but there are incentives. Direct access to most physicians is possible if costs of the visit are paid privately (the Czech Republic, Denmark, Finland, France, Iceland, Ireland, Malta, Slovakia);

3. Partial gatekeeping system in place. Patients need a referral for only a selection of physicians (Hungary, Latvia, Poland, Sweden);

4. Full gatekeeping system in place. A referral is normally required to access most specialist physicians (Bulgaria, Estonia, Italy, Lithuania, the Netherlands, Norway, Portugal, Romania, Slovenia, Spain, the United Kingdom).

Skill-mix of primary care providers

The organization of primary care can facilitate or hinder coordination, both within primary care and between primary and secondary care. Primary care may be organized around single-handed or group practices, or broader groupings including primary care and secondary care specialists. Countries with centralized responsibilities for primary care have more solo practices than decentralized primary care systems. In Austria, Bulgaria, the Czech Republic, Hungary, Latvia and Slovakia large majorities of general practices are single-handed. In almost half of the countries primary care is dominated by solo practices. The opposite is true for Finland, Lithuania, Poland, Portugal, Spain, Sweden and Turkey, where almost all GPs are working in group or mixed practices. Mixed practices with GPs and medical specialists are seen in Cyprus (20%), Germany (9%), Greece (20%), Latvia (8%), Lithuania (80%), Malta (20%), Romania (7%) and Slovenia (20%). They occur in 1% or fewer cases in the Czech Republic, Finland, Hungary, Spain and the United Kingdom. GPs working in group or mixed practices have more face-to-face meetings with other primary care providers, and offer more special sessions or clinics for specific patient groups, than single-handed general practices, thereby facilitating coordination of care.

The role of nurses in primary care is limited in most countries. Only in 12 countries do nurses provide health education in primary care, and the provision of nurse-led diabetes clinics is even less common (occurring in only five countries). Only in Denmark, the Netherlands, the United Kingdom, Sweden and Turkey are both types of nurse-led service offered.

Cooperation of primary and secondary care and public health

Cooperation between primary care providers and medical specialists is very limited in Austria, Bulgaria, Cyprus, Germany, Hungary, Iceland, Ireland, Norway, Portugal, Romania, Slovakia and Turkey. This may result from mutual competition when, as in Germany, medical specialists also work in primary care. In other countries, the most common model of cooperation is the provision of clinical lessons by medical specialists for GPs. The most extensive forms of cooperation exist in Sweden (including relocated specialist care, joint consultations and clinical lessons). GPs in the majority of countries do not regularly ask telephone advice from medical specialists (only in 13 countries).

Coordination between primary care and public health is underdeveloped in most countries. Only in 10 countries is primary care data routinely used to identify health policy priorities. However, community health surveys to improve the quality of primary care are conducted in all countries except Luxembourg, and regular nationwide surveys are undertaken in Belgium, Estonia, the Netherlands, Romania, Spain, Sweden, Switzerland and the United Kingdom.

Overall coordination of primary care by country

Fig. 3.3 summarizes all indicators on coordination by country (see Appendix II for the applied scoring system). Compared to the other aspects of service delivery, scores on coordination are generally low. Furthermore the variation between countries is considerably higher than the other aspects. What especially contributed to the low scores is the collaboration between primary care and secondary care and the scale and skill-mix of primary care practices. Currently, the dominant mode of general practice continues to be the single-handed practice, although in many countries group practices are increasing. Solo practice has limited possibilities for delivering integrated care.

Combining all measures of coordination, Fig. 3.3 shows that Sweden, the Netherlands, Lithuania, Denmark, Greece, Poland, the United Kingdom, Slovenia, Spain and Malta have the highest level of coordination of care. This is lowest in Austria, Germany, Slovakia, Bulgaria, Hungary, Cyprus, Romania, Norway, Ireland, Iceland and Turkey. All other countries have a medium level of coordination of care.

Fig. 3.3

Total coordination of primary care score by country (scale 1 (low) – 3 (high))

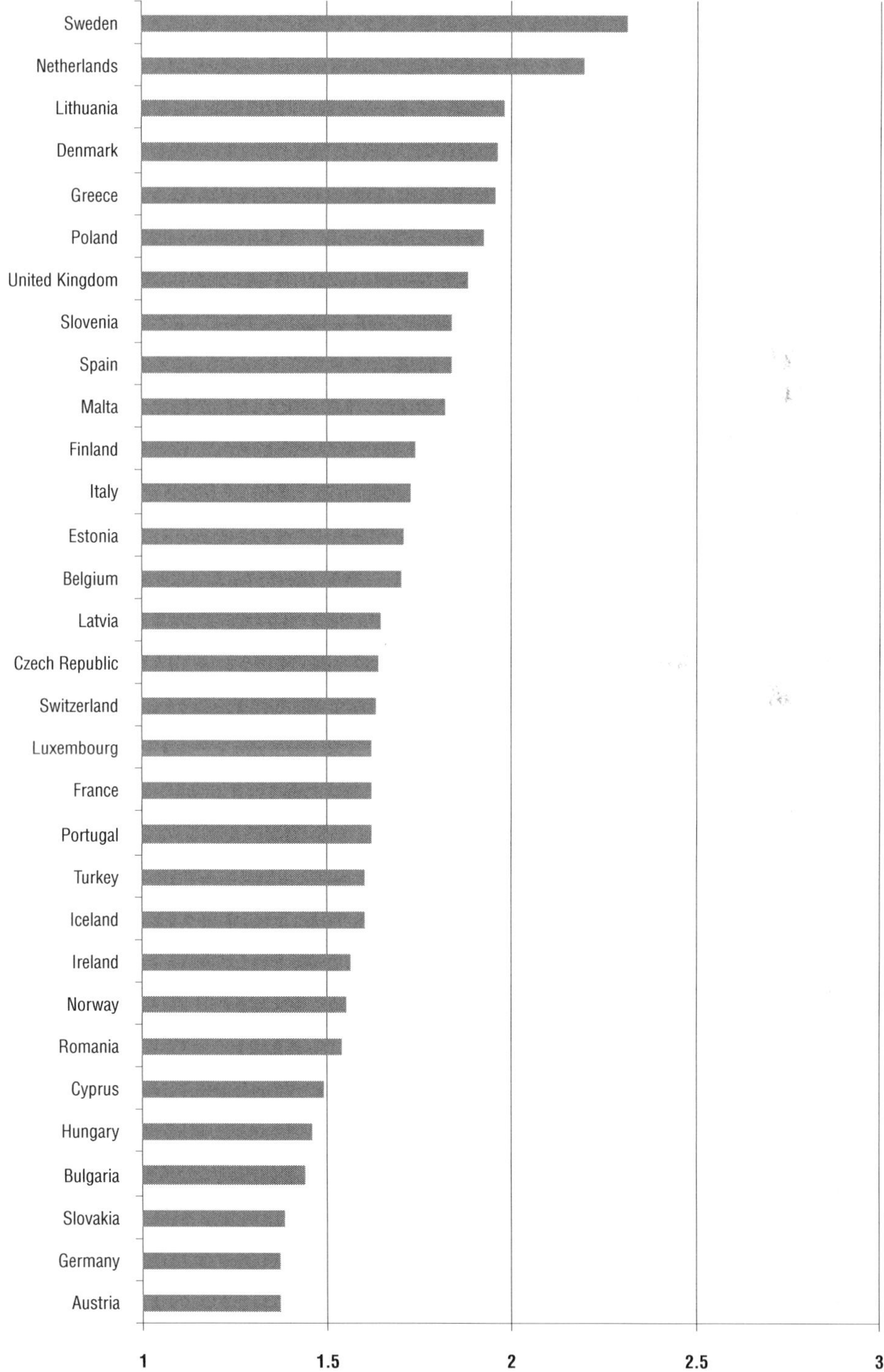

3.4 Comprehensiveness of services provided in primary care

The broader the range of services that are offered to patients in primary care, the smaller the dependency on secondary care services, and the stronger primary care is. Possibilities to provide services are related to the availability of medical equipment in primary care practices.

The range of services offered includes the following domains of care: first-contact care and triage; diagnostic services, treatment and follow-up care; medical technical procedures; prevention and health promotion; and mother, child and reproductive health care.

This section deals with the important features of comprehensiveness of primary care in each of the countries analysed (see Appendix I for an overview of features and indicators).

Table 3.4 provides an overview of results of the comprehensiveness of primary care by country.

Primary care facilities are generally well equipped across Europe, although in Austria, Hungary, Italy, Luxembourg, Malta, Poland, Romania, Slovakia and Slovenia items such as gynaecological speculums, peak flow meters, ECG recorders, urine strips, instruments for stitching wounds or infant scales are not always in place. The diversity of problems for which patients can be helped in primary care (such as a severely coughing child, contraception problems, alcohol addiction) is highest in Bulgaria, Denmark, Finland, France, Hungary, Norway, Poland, Portugal and Sweden.

GPs often provide treatment and follow-up care for a broader scope of conditions in countries with more solo practices, although this may be a function of demographics; for example, in remote areas, GPs are more likely to work solo and offer a fuller range of services. Other frequently visited specialist providers for treatment and follow-up care are cardiologists, rheumatologists, gastroenterologists, psychiatrists, pulmonologists, oncologists, internists, endocrinologists, diabetologists and geriatricians. Overall, GPs handle more than 90% of their total patient contacts without referral in Denmark, Estonia, Finland, Iceland, the Netherlands, Norway, Portugal, Spain and Switzerland.

Table 3.4

Comprehensiveness of primary care services, overview of selection of results by country

Country	Availability of equipment in PC facilities (9 items)[1]	GP involvement in first contact care (10 health problems)[2]	Other specialties involved in first contact care (for 10 health problems)[3]	GP involvement in treatment / follow-up care (9 diseases)[4]	Other specialties involved in treatment/follow-up care (9 diseases)[3]	% of total patient contacts handled solely by GPs without referral	GP or G/PC nurse involvement in medical technical procedures (10 activities)[5]	Other specialties providing medical technical procedures	GP involvement in preventive care (11 activities)[6]	Other specialties providing preventive care[3]	GP involvement in individual health counselling (4 cases)	Other specialties providing counselling[3]	GPs usually involved in group wise health education	Total level of comprehensiveness of PC services[8]
Austria	7/9	1/10	GYN; PAED; PSYT	9/9	INT; PSYT	70	0/10	GYN; IN; OPH; ORT; SUR	4/11	GYN; INT; PAED	4/4	INT; PSYT	No, incidentally	L
Belgium	9/9	7/10	GYN; NEU; OTO; PAED; PSYL; PSYT	9/9	CAR; END; GAS; GER; NUR; ONC; PSYT; PUL; REU	–	6/10	ANE; DER; GYN; OPH; ORT; PHY; SUR	8/11	CAR; GYN; INT; OB; OCT; PAED; SCN	4/4	DIE; NU; PCN; PHT; PSYL; PSYT	No, incidentally	M
Bulgaria	9/9	10/10	ENT; GYN; NEU; PSYT; SUR	9/9	CAR; END; GAS; NEU; PSYT; PUL; REU	87	4/10	DER; NUR; OPH; SUR	7/11	ALL; CAR; DER; GYN; INF; PAED; SUR	4/4	END; PSYT; PUL	Yes	H
Cyprus	8/9	0/10	CHE; ENT; GYN; NEU; PSYT	5/9	CAR; CHE; DIA; END; GAS; INT; ONC; PSYT; REU;	–	2/10	DER; GYN; OPH; ORT; POD; SUR	4/11	GYN; PAED	3/4	CAR; CHE; END; PSYT	–	L
Czech Republic	8/9	5/10	ADD; ENT; GYN; NEU; PAED; PSYT	5/9	CAR; DIA; GAS; INT; PSYT; PUL; REU	85	0/10	DER; GYN; INT; OPH; ORT; PUL; REU; SUR	5/11	CAR; DER; GER; GYN; INT; ONC; PAED; PUL; RAD	4/4	END; INT; PSYT; PUL	No	M
Denmark	8/9	9/10	ENT; ER; GYN; NEU; PAED; SPCL; PSYT; SW	7/9	CAR; END; GAS; HOS; INT; ONC; PAL; PSYL; PSYT; PUL; REU; SUR	90	2/10	ER; GYN; OPH; REU; SUR	9/11	ALL; ER; GYN; INF; INT; SPCL	3/4	DIE; PHN; PHY; SPCL	No	H
Estonia	9/9	7/10	ER; GYN; ONC; PSYT	9/9	CAR; END; GAS; NUR; ONC; PSYT; PUL; REU	92	1/10	GYN; OPH; REU; SUR; TR	6/11	ALL; CAR; DER; GYN; INF; MID; ONC; PAED	0/4	–	No, incidentally	H

Country	Finland	France	Germany	Greece	Hungary	Iceland	Ireland
Total level of comprehensiveness of PC services[8]	H	H	L	L	M	H	L
GPs usually involved in group wise health education	No, incidentally	No	No, incidentally	Yes	No	No, incidentally	No
Other specialties providing counselling[3]	DIE; INT; NU; PHY; PUL	DIE; END; GAS; PUL	INT; PSYL; PSYT; PUL	PATH	DIA; DIE; INT; SPN; PSYT; PUL	INT; PUL; NU	INT; SPN; PUL
GP involvement in individual health counselling (4 cases)	4/4	4/4	4/4	3/4	4/4	4/4	4/4
Other specialties providing preventive care[3]	GYN	ALL; CAR; DER; END; GYN; MID; OB; PAED; PUL; SPCL	ALL; DER; GYN; INT; MID; PAED; SUR; UR	GYN; PAED; PATH	DER; ER; GYN; INT; VE	CAR; DER; GYN; HCN; MID; NUR; OB; PAED; SPCL; SPN; VE	CAR; DER; ER; GYN; INT; OB; PAED; PHN; VE
GP involvement in preventive care (11 activities)[6]	6/11	11/11	4/11	4/11	5/11	2/11	4/11
Other specialties providing medical technical procedures	ANE; DER; GYN; OPH; INT; ORT; SUR	ADD; ER; DER; GYN; NUR; OPH; ORT; SUR	DER; GYN; INTOPH; ORT; SUR	PATH	ER; GYN; OPH; ORT; REU; SUR	DER; ER; GYN; OPH; ORT; POD; SUR	DER; ER; GYN; OPH; ORT; POD; REU; SUR
GP or G/PC nurse involvement in medical technical procedures (10 activities)[5]	10/10	3/10	4/10	4/10	1/10	4/10	2/10
% of total patient contacts handled solely by GPs without referral	93	81	77	–	80	93	–
Other specialties involved in treatment/follow-up care (9 diseases)[3]	CAR; GER; INT; ONC; PSYL; PSYT; PUL; REU; SUR	ADD; CAR; END; GAS; ONC; PAED; PSYL; PSYT; PUL; REU	CAR; DIA; GAS; NEU; ONC; PSYT; PUL; REU	PATH	CAR; DIA; GAS; GER; INT; ONC; PSYT; PUL; REU	CARD; END; GAS; GER; ONC; PSYT; PUL; REU; SUR	CAR; END; GAS; GER; INT; ONC; PSYT; PUL; REU; SUR
GP involvement in treatment / follow-up care (9 diseases)[4]	8/9	7/9	8/9	4/9	9/9	5/9	5/9
Other specialties involved in first contact care (for 10 health problems)[3]	CN; ENT; GYN; NEU; PAED; PSYL; PSYT; SPCL	ER; ENT; GAS; GYN; NEU; PAED; SPCL; PSYL; PSYT; SUR	ENT; GYN; NEU; PAED; PSYL; PSYT	–	ER; ENT; GYN; NEU; PAED; PSYL; PSYT; PUL; SUR	GYN; NEU; PAED; PSYT; SUR	GYN; OB; NEU; PAED; PSYT; SUR
GP involvement in first contact care (10 health problems)[2]	7/10	9/10	3/10	0/10	3/10	9/10	8/10
Availability of equipment in PC facilities (9 items)[1]	9/9	9/9	8/9	–	7/9	9/9	8/9

Country	Italy	Latvia	Lithuania	Luxembourg	Malta	Netherlands	Norway	Poland
Total level of comprehensiveness of PC services [8]	L	M	H	M	L	M	H	L
GPs usually involved in group wise health education	No, incidentally	No	Yes	No	–	No	No	No
Other specialties providing counselling [3]	PHN; PUL	END; NAR	CAR; END; PSYT; PUL	END; INT; NU; PSYT	–	PN	PHN; PN; SCN; SPCL	END; PHY; PSYT
GP involvement in individual health counselling (4 cases)	4/4	4/4	4/4	4/4	4/4	3/4	4/4	4/4
Other specialties providing preventive care [3]	ALL; GYN; LAB; MID; ONC; PAED; PHN	CAR; GYN; INF; INT; MID; PAED	CAR; GYN; INF; ONC; PAED; UR	ALL; CAR; DER; END; ER; GYN; INT; PAED	GYN; PAED	ENT; GYN; LAB; MID; PAED; PHN; SPCL	GYN; MID; PHN; RAD	ALL; CAR; DER; ER; GYN; INF; INT; OB; PAED; SUR
GP involvement in preventive care (11 activities) [6]	5/11	6/11	11/11	8/11	5/11	6/11	9/11	4/11
Other specialties providing medical technical procedures	DER; GYN; INT; NUR; OPH; ORT; SPN; SUR	GYN; NUR; OPH; SUR; TR	GYN; INT; OPH; SUR	DER; ER; GYN; OPH; ORT; REU; SPN; SUR	–	GYN; INT; OPH; ORT; PHY; SUR	DER; GYN; OPH; REU; SUR	DER; ER; GYN; INT; OPH; ORT; PAED; SUR
GP or G/PC nurse involvement in medical technical procedures (10 activities) [5]	1/10	1/10	4/10	2/10	4/10	8/10	5/10	0/10
% of total patient contacts handled solely by GPs without referral	–	16	70	–	–	96	95	–
Other specialties involved in treatment/follow-up care (9 diseases) [3]	CAR; DIA; GAS; INT; NUR; ONC; PSYT; PUL; REU	ADD; CAR; END; GAS; INT; NEU; ONC; PSYT; PUL; REU	CAR; END; GAS; INT; ONC; PSYT; PUL; REU	CAR; END; GAS; INT; ONC; PSYT; PUL; REU	–	CAR; DIA; INT; NHP; ONC; PSYL; PSYT; PUL; REU	CAR; GAS; INF; ONC; PSYL; PUL; REU	CAR; DIA; END; GAS; GER; INT; ORT; PSYT; PAL; PUL; REU
GP involvement in treatment / follow-up care (9 diseases) [4]	5/9	8/9	8/9	8/9	9/9	3/9	9/9	9/9
Other specialties involved in first contact care (for 10 health problems) [3]	GYN; NEU; ONC; PAED; PSYT	GYN; NAR; ONC; OTO; PSYT	GYN; PAED; PSYT	ER; ENT; GYN; NEU; PAED; PSYT	ER; GYN; PAED; PSYT; SW	ER; GYN; PSYL; SW	ER; CAR; CHE; GYN; SCN; SPCL; PSYT	END; ENT; GYN; OB; NEU; PAED; PSYT; SUR; SW
GP involvement in first contact care (10 health problems) [2]	6/10	5/10	10/10	5/10	9/10	9/10	7/10	4/10
Availability of equipment in PC facilities (9 items) [1]	4/9	9/9	9/9	7/9	6/9	8/9	9/9	6/9

Country	Portugal	Romania	Slovakia	Slovenia	Spain	Sweden	Switzerland
Availability of equipment in PC facilities (9 items) [1]	8/9	6/9	4/9	7/9	9/9	9/9	8/9
GP involvement in first contact care (10 health problems) [2]	9/10	8/10	5/10	5/10	5/10	7/10	5/10
Other specialties involved in first contact care (for 10 health problems) [3]	ENT; GYN; INT; NEU; PAED; PSYT; SUR	PAED; SPCL; PSYT	GYN; NEU; PAED; PSYT	GYN; PAED	GYN; NEU; ONC; OTO; PSYT	ENT; GYN; INT; PAED; PSYL; PSYT; SPCL; SUR; SW	ER; ENT; GYN; PAED; PSYT; SPCL
GP involvement in treatment / follow-up care (9 diseases) [4]	8/9	7/9	6/9	7/9	8/9	9/9	9/9
Other specialties involved in treatment/follow-up care (9 diseases) [3]	CAR; END; GAS; INT; ONC; PSYT; PUL; REU	CAR; DIA; GAS; INF; INT; PSYT; PUL; REU	CAR; DIA; GAS; INT; ONC; PSYT; PUL; REU	CAR; DIA; GAS; INF; ONC; PSYT; PUL; REU	CAR; END; GAS; ONC; PSYT; PAL; PUL; REU	CAR; GAS; GER; INF; INT; ONC; PSYL; PSYT; PAL; PUL; REU; SUR	CAM; CAR; END; GAS; GER; GYN; ONC; PUL; REU
% of total patient contacts handled solely by GPs without referral	94	35	72	80	94	80	99
GP or G/PC nurse involvement in medical technical procedures (10 activities) [5]	1/10	3/10	0/10	0/10	3/10	8/10	3/10
Other specialties providing medical technical procedures	DER; ER; GYN; OPH; ORT; SUR	–	DER; GYN; INT; OPH; ORT; REU; SUR	DER; GYN; OPH; ORT; SUR	DER; GYN; OB; OPH; REU; SUR; TR	ER; DER; GER; GYN; INT; NUR; OPH; SPCL; SUR	ANE; DER; GYN; NUR; OPH; ORT; PHY; RAD; REU; SUR; TR
GP involvement in preventive care (11 activities) [6]	10/11	5/11	5/11	5/11	6/11	6/11	7/11
Other specialties providing preventive care [3]	ALL; END; ER; GYN; INT; OCT; PAED; PUL	–	ALL; CAR; DER; GYN; INF; INT; OCT; PAED; SUR; VE	ALL; GYN; OB; ONC; SUR	ALL; CAR; OB; GYN; MID; PAED; PUL	ALL; ER; GYN; INT; MID; OCT; PAED; SPCL; UR	ALL; DER; ER; GYN; INF; MID; NUR; PHA; PAED; SCN; SPCL
GP involvement in individual health counselling (4 cases)	4/4	1/4	4/4	4/4	4/4	4/4	4/4
Other specialties providing counselling [3]	END; INT; PN; PSYT	PN	END; INT; PHY; PSYT; PUL	–	END; PHY; PUL; PSYT	PSYT; SW	CAR; DIE; END; SPCL; PSYT; PUL; UR
GPs usually involved in group wise health education	No, incidentally	–	No	Yes	No, incidentally	–	No
Total level of comprehensiveness of PC services [8]	H	L	L	L	H	M	M

Country	Availability of equipment in PC facilities (9 items)[1]	GP involvement in first contact care (10 health problems)[2]	Other specialties involved in first contact care (for 10 health problems)[3]	GP involvement in treatment / follow-up care (9 diseases)[4]	Other specialties involved in treatment/follow-up care (9 diseases)[3]	% of total patient contacts handled solely by GPs without referral	GP or G/PC nurse involvement in medical technical procedures (10 activities)[5]	Other specialties providing medical technical procedures	GP involvement in preventive care (11 activities)[6]	Other specialties providing preventive care[3]	GP involvement in individual health counselling (4 cases)	Other specialties providing counselling[3]	GPs usually involved in group wise health education	Total level of comprehensiveness of PC services[8]
Turkey	8/9	5/10	–	6/9	CAR; END; GAS; GER; INF; INT; ONC; PAED; PSYT; REU	–	4/10	DER; GYN; OPH; NUR; ORT; SUR	8/11	GYN; INT; PAED; SUR; UR	3/4	INT; PUL	Yes	M
United Kingdom	9/9	10/10	–	9/9	CAR; DIA; GAS; GER; NUR; PAL; PN; PUL; REU; SPN	–	4/10	ER; CHI; ER; OPH; OPT; ORT; REU ; SPCL; SUR	6/11	ALL; GUM; HV; MID; PHA; SPCL	4/4	DIE; SPCL	No	M

1 Number of items of equipment always or usually available in PC facilities from a list of 9 types of equipment: 1. infant scales; 2. glucose tests; 3. dressings/bandages; 4. otoscope; 5.ECG; 6. urine strips; 7. instruments for stitching wounds; 8. gynaecological speculum; 9. peak flow meter.
2 GPs always or usually involved in first contact care for (10 health problems): 1. child with severe cough; 2. child aged 8 with hearing problem; 3. woman aged 18 asking for oral contraception; 4. woman aged 20 for confirmation of pregnancy; 5. woman aged 35 with irregular menstruation; 6. woman aged 35 with psychosocial problems; 7. woman aged 50 with a lump in her breast; 8. man aged 28 with a first convulsion; 9. man with suicidal inclinations; 10. man aged 52 with alcohol addiction problems.
3 ADD = Addiction specialist; ALL = Allergologist; ANE = Anaesthesiologist; CAM = Complementary and alternative medicine; CAR = Cardiologist; NEU = Neurologist; CHE = Chest physician; CHI = Chiropodist; CN= Community nurse; DER = Dermatologist; DIA = Diabetologist; DIE = Dietician; ENT = Ear Nose Throat Specialist; END = Endocrinologist; ER = Emergency room of hospital; GAS = Gastroenterologist; GER = Geriatrician; GUM = GUM specialist; GYN=Gynaecologist; HCN = Home care nurse; HOS = Hospices; HV = Health visitors; INF = Infection specialist; INT = Specialist of Internal medicine; LAB = Laboratrician; MID = Midwife (ambulatory); NAR = Narcologist; NHP = Nursing home physician; NUR = Nurse; OB = Obstetrician; OCT = Occupational therapist; ONC = Oncologist; OPH = Ophthalmologist; OPT = Optometrician; ORT = Orthopaedist; OTO = Otorhinolaryngologist; PAED = Paediatrician; PAL = Palliative care specialist; PATH = Pathologist; PCN = Primary care/General practice nurse; PHA = Pharmacist; PHN = Public health nurse; PHT = Physiotherapist (ambulatory); PHY = Physiotherapist; POD = Podiatrist; PSYL = Psychologist; PSYT = psychiatrist; PUL = Pulmonologist; RAD = Radiologist; REU = Rheumatologist; SCN = School nurse or health station; SPCH = Speech therapist; DEN = Dentist; SPCL = Special clinic; SPN = Specialized nurse; SUR = Surgeon; SW = Social worker; TR = Traumatologist; UR = Urologist; VE = Venerologist.
4 GPs always or usually involved in treatment and follow-up care for (9 diseases): 1. Chronic bronchitis; 2. Peptic ulcer; 3. Congestive heart failure; 4. Pneumonia; 5. Uncomplicated diabetes type II; 6. Rheumatoid arthritis; 7. Mild depression; 8. Cancer (in need of palliative care); 9. Patients admitted to a nursing home/convalescent home.
5 GPs or G/PC practice nurses always or usually involved in treatment and follow-up care for (10 activities): 1. Wedge resection of ingrown toenail; 2. Removal of sebaceous cyst from hairy scalp; 3. Wound suturing; 4. Excision of warts; 5. Insertion of IUD; 6. Removal of rusty spot from the cornea; 7. Fundoscopy; 8. Joint injection; 9. Strapping an ankle; 10. Setting up an intravenous infusion.
6 GPs always or usually involved in the following preventive care activities (11 activities): 1. Immunization for tetanus; 2. Allergy vaccinations; 3. Testing for sexually transmitted diseases; 4. Screening for HIV/AIDS; 5. Influenza vaccination for high-risk groups; 6. Cervical cancer screening; 7. Breast cancer screening; 8. Cholesterol level checking; 9. Family planning/contraceptive care; 10. Routine antenatal care (in line with national scheme); 11. Routine paediatric surveillance for children up to 4 years.
7 GPs always or usually involved in individual health promotion counselling (4 cases): 1. Counselling in case of obesity; 2. Counselling in case of poor physical activity; 3. Counselling in case of smoking cessation; 4. Counselling in case of problematic alcohol
8 H= Relatively high level of comprehensiveness of PC services; M= Relatively medium level of comprehensiveness of PC services; L= Relatively low level of comprehensiveness of PC services. Categories are made based on the relative distribution of data for all indicators of this dimension of the PC Monitor Instrument (which are not all mentioned in this table).

Medical technical procedures are most frequently carried out by GPs and primary care nurses in Belgium, Finland, the Netherlands, Norway and Sweden. Other providers who often perform typically primary care medical technical procedures are surgeons, ophthalmologists, gynaecologists, dermatologists, orthopaedists, rheumatologists, emergency room specialists, internists and nurses.

Preventive activities are provided by a large variety of providers in the majority of countries. Preventive care is frequently provided by gynaecologists, paediatricians, allergists, internists, cardiologists, dermatologists, midwives, emergency room specialists, infection specialists, obstetricians and special clinics, in addition to GPs.

Overall comprehensiveness of services by country

A summary of all comprehensiveness scores by country is presented in Fig. 3.4. With all measures combined there are only small differences between countries. Primary care services are most comprehensive in Lithuania, Norway, Bulgaria, Belgium, the United Kingdom, Spain, Finland, Sweden, Portugal and France. A more narrow profile was found in Slovakia, Italy, Greece, Cyprus, Romania, Hungary, Poland, the Netherlands, Slovenia, the Czech Republic and Austria. The other countries are in an intermediate position regarding comprehensiveness of primary care services.

3.5 Overall service delivery in primary care

In Fig. 3.5 the countries' positions on all dimensions of the primary care services delivery process have been taken together. Denmark, Spain and the United Kingdom have a high accessibility of primary care, provide a relatively high level of continuity and coordination of primary care, and provide the most comprehensive scope of primary care services. Countries where accessibility, continuity, coordination and comprehensiveness of primary care are somewhat less consistent are Estonia, Lithuania, Portugal and to a lesser degree (medium level) the Czech Republic, Finland and Poland. Austria and Cyprus have a relatively weak primary care services delivery process (considering all four dimensions). Consistency is even lower (weak/medium) in Bulgaria, Italy, Luxembourg, Romania and Turkey, and to a lesser degree (medium level) in Greece, Ireland, Malta and Switzerland. The least consistency among the dimensions of service delivery was found in the remaining 11 countries.

Fig. 3.4

Total comprehensiveness of primary care score by country (scale 1 (low) – 3 (high))

Overall, the scores of the four dimensions of the primary care services delivery process show no associations with each other. Each of the primary care structure dimensions is positively associated with primary care accessibility (Spearman's correlation values range from 0.37 [p-value 0.04] for access – economic conditions to 0.54 [p-value 0.00] for access – governance). In addition, coordination of primary care is positively associated with primary care governance and primary care workforce development. The Spearman's correlation values are 0.38 (p-value 0.03) and 0.41 (p-value 0.02) respectively.

Fig. 3.5

Overall (high/medium/low) level of accessibility, continuity and coordination of primary care by country

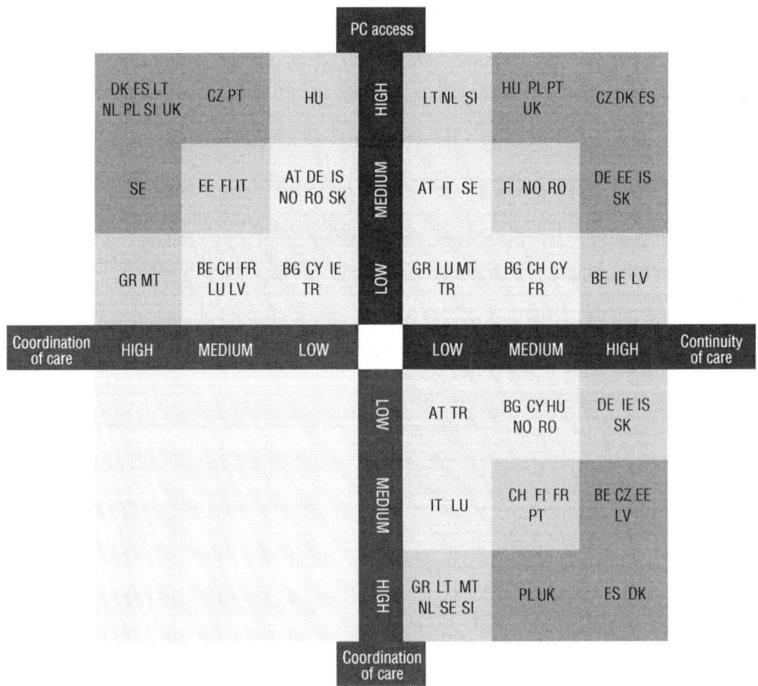

Key: AT – Austria; BE – Belgium; BG – Bulgaria; CH – Switzerland; CY – Cyprus; CZ – Czech Rep.; DE – Germany; DK – Denmark; EE – Estonia; ES – Spain; FI – Finland; FR – France; GR – Greece; HU – Hungary; IE – Ireland; IS – Iceland; IT – Italy; LT – Lithuania; LU – Luxembourg; LV – Latvia; MT – Malta; NL – Netherlands; NO – Norway; PL – Poland; PT – Portugal; RO – Romania; SE – Sweden; SI – Slovenia; SK – Slovakia; TR – Turkey; UK – United Kingdom.

3.6 Conclusions

This chapter has characterized the delivery of services in primary care by the breadth and comprehensiveness of the package of services delivered, how services are accessed by patients and the functions of continuity and coordination of care.

- Obstacles to access were related to shortage of GPs which were usually more perceptible in rural areas than in towns and cities.

- Geographical equality is not optimal in most countries. In general, access outside normal office hours is differently organized and in most countries typically non-practice-based, which may be unfavourable for continuity of care.

- Home-bound patients in countries where GPs rarely make home visits may experience difficulties in receiving the care they need. Although most countries had no financial barriers for visiting a GP, home visits and prescriptions were more often subject to private payments.

- Major conditions for continuity of care are well-kept medical records for patients and GPs being responsible (and accountable) for care provided to a defined practice population. Such "patients' lists" were mandatory for all patients in two-thirds of the countries. In general, differences between countries on continuity were modest.

- On coordination, differences were larger and countries performed less well. A gatekeeping system was operational in only a quarter of the countries, although in others a partial gatekeeping system was in place, or at least there were incentives for patients to achieve the same effect. Solo practice, which is less favourable for coordination, was still the dominant mode of practice in almost half of the countries. Collaboration between GPs and medical specialists was an area for improvement in many countries, and the links between primary care and public health were poorly developed.

- In the countries where GPs had a strong role as the doctor of first contact they treated more than 90% of all patient contacts without referral. Regarding the provision of medical procedures and prevention the variation was large; these task domains were less developed.

- No association was found between the four dimensions of service delivery explained in this chapter. But dimensions of structure (governance, economic conditions and workforce; dealt with in the previous chapter) were associated with access and coordination.

References

Hart JT (1971). The inverse care law. *The Lancet*, 1(7696):405–412.

Hill AP, Freeman GK (2011). *Promoting continuity of care in general practice.* London, Royal College of General Practitioners.

Huibers L et al. (2009). Out-of-hours care in western countries: assessment of different organizational models. *BMC Health Service Research*, 9:105.

Pascoe SW, Neal RD, Allgar VL (2004). Open-access versus bookable appointment systems: survey of patients attending appointments with general practitioners. *British Journal of General Practice*, 1(54):367–369.

Chapter 4

Diversity of primary care systems analysed

Dionne Kringos, Wienke Boerma, Yann Bourgueil, Thomas Cartier, Toni Dedeu, Toralf Hasvold, Allen Hutchinson, Margus Lember, Marek Oleszczyk, Danica Rotar Pavlič

This chapter analyses differences between countries and explains why countries differ regarding the structure and process of primary care. The components of primary care strength that are used in the analyses are health policy-making, workforce development and in the care process itself (see Fig. 1.1 in chapter 1). The explanations will be sought in the efficiency of primary care; societal, political and economic determinants; and the contribution of strong primary care to health system performance in general.

4.1 Diversity in structural aspects

Countries differed in *governance of primary care* because official visions on the future direction of primary care were not always well articulated or were even absent. Most countries had important primary care functions (e.g. priority setting, supply planning) decentralized to regional or local authorities. Quality of care is safeguarded by minimum standards in most countries, including professional education, clinical guidelines and patient rights. However, in several countries these standards are not well developed: exceptions to official training policies are sometimes applied in countries allowing nonspecialized physicians to work in primary care. Furthermore rules regarding continuing medical education are often absent. General practice guidelines are often made by medical specialists, the Ministry of Health or adapted from foreign guidelines. The breadth, quality and effective implementation of policies can therefore be largely improved in many countries.

In *economic conditions* a clear east–west divide was observed, especially regarding the relative level of health expenditures, which is notably lower in the eastern European countries, and income of providers. The income of primary care providers in eastern Europe is often much lower than the income of medical specialists, which also limits the professional status of primary care providers. Furthermore, primary care providers' remuneration systems are in almost all European countries topped up by various performance-related financial incentives to influence physician behaviour. Self-employment with a contract is the predominant employment status of GPs in Europe.

A major issue on *workforce development* was an ageing primary care workforce and potential shortages within 10 years' time. Only half of the countries have data available from studies on primary care workforce capacity needs and development in the future. On average, one-fifth of all medical graduates choose to enrol in postgraduate GP training in Europe. GPs are rather well organized: national organizations for GPs exist in all countries (except Iceland). For nurses, on the contrary, this is rarely the case.

The *overall ranking of the structure of primary care* is based on the scores of all primary care structure dimensions. These dimensions are positively associated with one another, which means they are related to one another's performance (Spearman's correlation values were 0.49 for governance and workforce development with economic conditions [$p = 0.01$] and 0.55 [$p = 0.00$] for governance with workforce development). As a result, the strength of primary care at structure level can be summarized by one score, which is presented for each country in Fig. 4.1 and in the first column of Table 4.1.

Countries with the highest ranking on structural aspects are the United Kingdom, the Netherlands, Spain, Portugal, Denmark and Slovenia. In the tail of the ranking are Iceland, Luxembourg and Cyprus.

Table 4.1

Overview of variables by country

Country	PC structure strength[1] (2009/10)	Access: PC process strength[1] (2009/10)	Continuity of care: PC process strength[1] (2009/10)	Coordination of care: PC process strength[1] (2009/10)	Comprehensiveness: PC process strength[1] (2009/10)	GPs involvement first contact care[2] (1993)	GDP per capita (PPP USD) (1993)	% growth in GDP per capita (PPP USD) 1993–2009	Years left party government dominance 1993–2008	Type of health care system (2010)	% population agree government should take more responsibility providing welfare (N;Year)	% population prefers children to take care of parent(s) in case of ill health (N) 2007	% population agree healthy impact science & technology (N) 2010
Austria	2.22	2.27	2.19	1.38	2.33	2.95	21 563.30	80.02	4.75	SHI	n.a.	46.06 (1003)	64.80 (517)
Belgium	2.21	2.13	2.38	1.70	2.53	3.01	20 482.00	77.29	7.75	SHI	n.a.	37.95 (1033)	57.84 (529)
Bulgaria	2.14	2.15	2.33	1.44	2.54	1.74	5030.37	175.72	5.14	TRANS	53.24 (971;1997)	79.59 (1014)	44.36 (505)
Cyprus	1.91	2.11	2.32	1.49	2.19	n.a.	13 683.20	125.45	4.25	NHS	51.58 (1043;2006)	65.43 (486)	56.80 (250)
Czech Republic	2.14	2.35	2.41	1.64	2.33	2.28	10 500.20	143.62	6.25	TRANS	55.97 (1147;1998)	65.04 (1027)	39.12 (524)
Denmark	2.38	2.46	2.43	1.96	2.40	3.49	20 439.60	84.55	6.25	NHS	n.a.	21.97 (1006)	64.23 (520)
Estonia	2.29	2.21	2.42	1.71	2.41	2.06	5645.03	248.86	4.75	TRANS	63.80 (1011;1996)	59.52 (1003)	52.86 (490)
Finland	2.31	2.20	2.32	1.74	2.51	3.00	16 868.40	109.06	6.50	NHS	31.49 (975;1996)	31.12 (1041)	64.62 (537)
France	2.16	2.06	2.33	1.63	2.47	3.08	18 715.10	79.93	5.25	SHI	28.06 (998;2006)	37.32 (1096)	63.57 (516)
Germany	2.20	2.25	2.38	1.38	2.34	2.82	20 756.00	75.07	8.50	SHI	46.97 (2014;1997)	53.78 (1523)	36.02 (769)
Greece	2.10	2.08	2.25	1.96	2.17	2.47	13 738.30	115.58	10.50	NHS	n.a.	86.26 (1012)	46.88 (529)
Hungary	2.08	2.34	2.33	1.46	2.29	2.75	8066.11	151.82	9.00	TRANS	65.99 (638;1998)	70.18 (1006)	49.52 (523)
Iceland	1.77	2.28	2.40	1.60	2.42	3.10	21 764.60	69.06	2.00	NHS	n.a.	n.a.	64.41 (236)
Ireland	2.20	1.96	2.38	1.57	2.36	3.48	14 973.70	171.79	2.75	NHS	n.a.	41.74 (1011)	65.08 (504)
Italy	2.33	2.27	2.31	1.73	2.13	3.08	19 283.90	68.17	5.07	NHS	44.11 (984;2005)	50.89 (1067)	41.47 (516)
Latvia	2.14	2.15	2.38	1.65	2.41	1.96	4910.72	234.72	4.50	TRANS	61.41 (1192;1996)	70.55 (1012)	41.77 (486)
Lithuania	2.27	2.29	2.30	1.98	2.56	1.71	6292.90	175.04	8.50	TRANS	50.90 (998;1997)	74.17 (1026)	46.33 (518)
Luxembourg	1.90	2.03	2.31	1.63	2.42	2.63	36 469.70	129.84	5.50	SHI	n.a.	45.28 (360)	68.00 (250)

Indicator	Malta	Netherlands	Norway	Poland	Portugal	Romania	Slovakia	Slovenia	Spain	Sweden	Switzerland	Turkey	United Kingdom	Source:
% population agree healthy impact science & technology (N) 2010	58.61 (244)	54.60 (522)	65.34 (479)	43.55 (535)	45.42 (513)	53.28 (533)	40.08 (499)	47.72 (505)	62.98 (497)	76.83 (492)	60.00 (490)	66.10 (472)	61.39 (663)	TNS Opinion & Social, 2010
% population prefers children to take care of parent(s) in case of ill health (N) 2007	54.34 (495)	22.81 (1004)	n.a.	84.38 (1031)	57.96 (1068)	78.62 (1043)	74.91 (1084)	45.21 (1033)	57.80 (993)	14.82 (985)	n.a.	81.92 (1001)	44.58 (1283)	TNS Opinion & Social & TNS, 2007
% population agree government should take more responsibility providing welfare (N;Year)	n.a.	36.41 (1041;2006)	29.95 (1122;1996)	41.94 (1111;1997)	n.a.	47.77 (1187;1998)	68.12 (1076;1998)	52.86 (997;1995)	51.38 (1162;1995)	12.85 (1004;1996)	16.34 (1181;1996)	45.93 (1868;1996)	27.23 (1032;2006)	World Values Survey Association, 2009
Type of health care system (2010)	NHS	SHI	NHS	TRANS	NHS	TRANS	TRANS	TRANS	NHS	NHS	SHI	SHI	NHS	European Observatory on Health Systems and Policies, 2011
Years left party government dominance 1993–2008	2.00	5.50	8.75	7.25	8.75	8.75	4.50	8.00	8.25	12.00	4.00	4.00	11.50	Armingeon et al., 2010; Akman, pers. comm. 2011 (for Turkey)
% growth in GDP per capita (PPP USD) 1993–2009	90.11	106.44	168.94	226.18	101.90	209.64	218.18	142.95	119.42	90.29	76.19	169.46	98.70	WHO Regional Office for Europe, 2011
GDP per capita (PPP USD) (1993)	13 052.30	19 703.20	20 901.90	5795.92	12 342.70	4611.19	7191.46	11 168.20	14 652.40	19 642.20	25 667.10	5072.25	17 692.70	WHO Regional Office for Europe, 2011
GPs involvement first contact care[2] (1993)	2.80	3.67	3.28	2.27	3.22	2.36	n.a.	2.87	3.20	2.83	2.88	2.02	3.51	Boerma et al., 1997; Sciortino, 2002 (for Malta)
Comprehensiveness: PC process strength[1] (2009/10)	2.38	2.32	2.55	2.29	2.47	2.20	1.98	2.32	2.51	2.49	2.42	2.36	2.52	Kringos et al., 2013a
Coordination of care: PC process strength[1] (2009/10)	1.82	2.20	1.56	1.92	1.62	1.55	1.39	1.84	1.84	2.32	1.63	1.61	1.88	Kringos et al., 2013a
Continuity of care: PC process strength[1] (2009/10)	2.17	2.26	2.36	2.33	2.35	2.33	2.39	2.30	2.43	2.25	2.37	2.15	2.37	Kringos et al., 2013a
Access: PC process strength[1] (2009/10)	2.17	2.38	2.25	2.35	2.34	2.26	2.27	2.47	2.44	2.17	2.17	2.05	2.40	Kringos et al., 2013a
PC structure strength[1] (2009/10)	2.12	2.50	2.27	2.12	2.41	2.31	2.02	2.36	2.43	2.23	2.04	2.27	2.52	Kringos et al., 2013a
Country	Malta	Netherlands	Norway	Poland	Portugal	Romania	Slovakia	Slovenia	Spain	Sweden	Switzerland	Turkey	United Kingdom	Source:

1 Scale ranges from 1 (low PC orientation) to 3 (high PC orientation).
2 Scale ranges from 1 (low involvement) to 4 (high involvement).

4.2 Diversity in the process of care delivery

Table 4.1 also provides the consolidated scores for the *strength of the process of primary care*, in terms of access, continuity, coordination and comprehensiveness of care. Denmark, Spain and the United Kingdom have a relatively strong primary care orientation on all process dimensions. Countries where this is somewhat inconsistent (high/medium) are Estonia, Lithuania and Portugal, and to a lesser degree (medium level) the Czech Republic, Finland and Poland. Austria and Cyprus have a relatively low primary care orientation on all process dimensions. Less consistency is found (low/medium) in Bulgaria, Italy, Luxembourg, Romania and Turkey, and to a lesser degree (medium level) Greece, Ireland, Malta and Switzerland. In the remaining 11 countries consistency among the process dimensions is lowest.

Concerning *accessibility,* large geographical inequalities in availability of GPs within countries are found across Europe, with remote areas often facing shortages. In almost half of the countries, patients often need to pay part of the costs of a GP contact, which may contradict official policies in favour of free access. Organizational arrangements to facilitate access leave ample room for improvement, particularly considering telephone and e-mail consultations, appointment systems, and offering consultations for special patient groups. Also, the chance of receiving a GP home visit differs greatly across Europe. In many countries, after-hours primary care services are organized through various parallel arrangements.

Though longitudinal *continuity of care* is relatively high in most countries, in some countries GPs have relatively large patient lists (e.g. Austria, Finland, Germany and the Netherlands). Improvements can be made in informational and interpersonal continuity of care, for example by offering primary care providers adequate software and training to use it. Practice computers can be used for multiple purposes, such as supporting public health functions, information exchange with peers and medical record-keeping. This equipment is often lacking. Where data exist, patients are least satisfied with primary care providers' communication skills and consultation duration (e.g. in Germany, the United Kingdom and Lithuania).

Fig. 4.1
Ranking of countries on the combined scores for structural aspects of primary care

In respect to *coordination of care,* modes of referral systems are in place across Europe. In several countries patients need a referral to be able to visit physicians outside primary care (except for emergencies). In some countries patients have direct access to most types of physician, while in others such direct access is possible if the costs of the visit are paid privately. The system of population-based registered patients (patient lists) is generally not used in Austria, Belgium, Cyprus, France, Germany, Ireland, Luxembourg, Malta, Sweden and Switzerland. Solo practice is the dominant mode of practice in almost half of the countries. Cooperation and coordination between primary and secondary care are problematic in many countries. In general, nurses have limited tasks in primary care although there are some notable exceptions, for example the United Kingdom and Spain.

Data on *comprehensiveness of care* show that the first-contact role of GPs is most developed in the countries where GPs are gatekeepers. In countries with many solo GPs, follow-up care is provided for a broader scope of conditions than in countries where group practices are more prevalent. In group practices more of these tasks may be delegated to other professionals in the team. Primary care practices are generally well equipped across Europe. In a few countries primary care nurses carry out medical technical procedures. Preventive care activities are provided by a large variety of providers in the majority of countries, including GPs. Overall, the highest level of comprehensiveness of primary care services exists in Belgium, Bulgaria, Finland, France, Lithuania, Norway, Portugal, Spain, Sweden and the United Kingdom.

4.3 Diversity in the overall strength of primary care

By taking data on all dimensions presented in the previous chapters together, including a general weighting procedure, an overall score for the strength of primary care in each country could be computed. In Fig. 4.2 countries have been divided into three groups, with respectively a low, medium and high score on primary care orientation, as measured by the indicators of the primary care structure and process (Kringos et al., 2013a).

Fig. 4.2

Variation in the overall strength of primary care in Europe

Countries where primary care is relatively strong are: Portugal and Spain, the countries around the North Sea (Belgium, the United Kingdom, the Netherlands and Denmark), Slovenia, and three countries in north-eastern Europe (Lithuania, Estonia and Finland). Primary care systems in central Europe are relatively weak, in particular in Slovakia, Austria and Hungary, and also in south-eastern Europe and Turkey.

Fig. 4.3

Overview of efficiency scores on relationships between (A) structure–process and (B) process–outcome

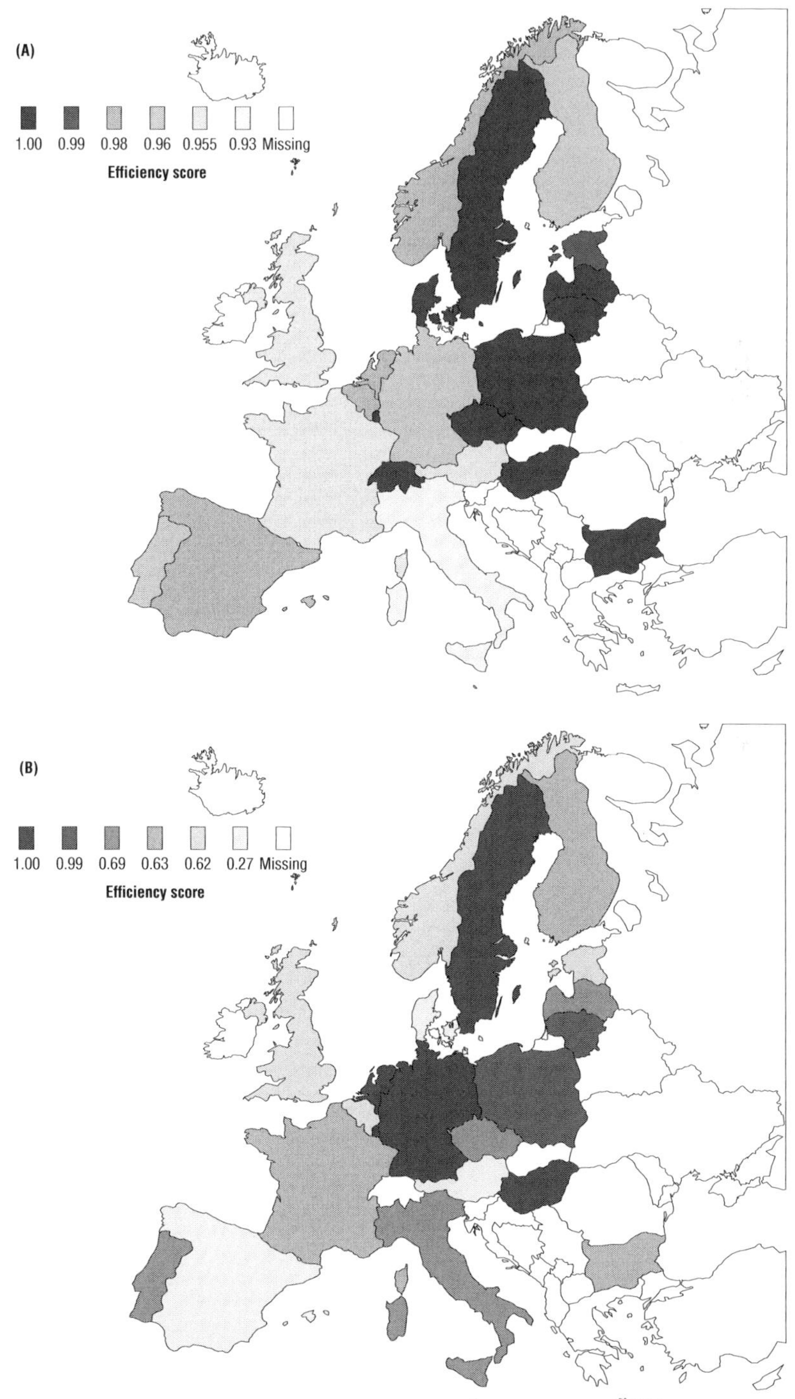

4.4 The efficiency of primary care

Data from the PHAMEU study have been used for an analysis of the efficiency of the organization of primary care, which is one of the outcome dimensions in the conceptual framework (Pelone et al., 2013). In this analysis countries have been compared, first, on the efficient use of their structure of primary care for the delivery of primary care services; and, second, on how efficiently quality of care was delivered. The focus has been on two types of relationship:

- The relationship between the three structure dimensions and the four process dimensions of primary care; and

- The relationship between the four process dimensions and quality of care.

The technical efficiency analysis performed included a subset of 22 countries, with the aim of assessing the mix and type of structure dimensions used by countries to obtain their achieved level of process dimensions. Fig. 4.3 shows the results of the efficiency analysis using Data Envelopment Analysis (score 1 = relatively most efficient).

The comparison between the strength of the countries' primary care system with their relative efficiency (in organizing primary care as a whole) showed that some of the countries with strong primary care are not among the most efficient systems, in relative terms. Only a few countries with a relatively strong primary care system were also relatively efficient: the Netherlands, Portugal, Finland, Lithuania and Estonia. In contrast, there were countries with a relatively weak primary care system but that were relatively efficient: Luxembourg, Bulgaria and Hungary. This finding suggests that maximizing the single functions of primary care without taking into account the coherence within the system is not sufficient if policy-makers aim to achieve both efficiency and strong primary care.

Overall, the results suggest that, to improve primary care efficiency, it is important to focus on strengthening access and coordination of care, and the economic resources available for primary care (Pelone et al., 2013). However, if policy-makers strengthen all aspects of primary care structure and process, this will not necessarily increase the efficiency of the overall health care system.

4.5 The role of wealth, culture, type of health care system and politics

To clarify the role of the broad societal context in the development of primary care systems we tried to answer the question why, in some countries, access and quality of primary care are better and a broader package of services is offered to patients than in others. It has been suggested that the outcome of the continuing process of primary care development is a result of political will, applied resources, public engagement and a facilitating health care system context (Groenewegen & Delnoij, 2003). Sidel and Sidel (1977) have argued that primary care is a reflection of a society's economic, social, political and cultural history and the general structure of the health care system.

With PHAMEU data, empirical evidence has been sought for these notions, in particular, by explaining why countries differ in their primary care structure and primary care services delivery process because of political-economic factors, cultural values and the type of health care system. For this analysis the following data were taken from other sources: (growth in) national income; the political orientation of a country's government; the prevailing values among inhabitants; and the type of health care system. Table 4.1 provides an overview of the value and position of each country on the variables included in this analysis.

International variation in the overall strength of primary care is related to differences in wealth, political composition of the government, prevailing values, and type of health care system.

Wealthier countries tend to have a weaker primary care structure and less accessibility of primary care services compared to less wealthy countries. On the other hand, *transitional countries* in eastern Europe have used their growth in national income to strengthen the accessibility and continuity of primary care. Countries that have been governed by a predominantly *left-wing government* over the past years typically have a stronger primary care structure, accessibility and coordination of primary care. It was also found that countries with a *social security-based system* have lower accessibility and continuity of primary care than do countries with NHS systems (Kringos et al., 2013b). This could be the result of a lack of a gatekeeping system and use of co-payments to control health care use in most SHI systems. The opposite is true for transitional systems in central and eastern Europe. This is likely the result of a difference in history, by which transitional countries, against a background of state-dominated centralized health care systems, had a strong wish to organize health care totally differently. Finally, it was found that *cultural values* affect all aspects of primary care. Cultural values refers to typical governmental responsibility to distribute welfare (as opposed to individual responsibility); the preference for family-based care over professional care utilization; and values on the impact of science and technology on health.

The combination of results on all three values showed that these values affect both primary care structure and primary care services delivery (see also Kringos et al., 2013b). These results suggest that the development of stronger primary care systems would require the mobilization of multiple leverage points, policy options and political will, and that prevailing values in a specific country should be taken into consideration.

4.6 The contribution of strong primary care to health care system performance

Strategies to cope with current challenges in the health care sector often include the strengthening of the primary care level. With the PHAMEU data an answer has been sought to the question: do countries with relatively strong primary care have better overall health care system outcomes compared to countries with relatively weak primary care?

The relationship was tested between the strength of five primary care dimensions and key health care system performance indicators: health care spending, patient-perceived quality of care, potentially avoidable hospitalizations, population health and socioeconomic inequality (Kringos et al., 2013c). Table 4.2 shows the correlations of primary care and outcome variables.

Data presented in Table 4.2 provides some evidence that strong primary care in Europe is positively associated with improving population health, reducing socioeconomic inequalities in health and avoiding potentially unnecessary hospitalizations. However, it seemed that health spending during the first decade of the 2000s seemed to be higher in countries with relatively stronger primary care provision. This finding requires further investigation.

4.7 Conclusion and observations

In general, the following conclusions can be drawn:

- A major observation from the study of health care systems in Europe is their variability. Health care systems are differently funded and structured, and services are provided in diverse settings. The differences in the role of primary care are a prominent aspect of this variation.

- Strong primary care appeared to be conducive to reaching health care system goals. The structure of primary care, and access to, coordination and comprehensiveness of primary care are all critical aspects of primary care that reduce unnecessary hospitalizations for conditions that can also be treated in primary care. Population health is better in countries with relatively stronger primary care compared to countries with relatively weaker primary care.

Table 4.2

Correlation of primary care structure and process variables with outcome variables

OUTCOME	STRUCTURE of PC	Accessibility	Continuity	Coordination	Comprehensiveness
		PROCESS of PC			
Total health expenditure, year 2009 (US$ purchasing power parities (PPP), per capita) [a]	-0.01	-0.01	0.08	0.11	0.22
% change total health expenditure, years 2000–2009 (US$ PPP, per capita) [a]	0.04	0.02	0.12	-0.10	**-0.37**
% pop. rating quality of family doctors as "good", year 2007 [b]	-0.05	-0.06	-0.04	-0.14	0.04
Asthma admission rate per 100 000 pop., years 2007–2009 [c]	-0.23	-0.13	0.05	-0.24	**-0.36**
COPD admission rate per 100 000 pop., years 2007–2009 [c]	-0.15	-0.11	0.13	-0.28	-0.09
Diabetes admission rate per 100 000 pop., years 2007–2009 [c]	-0.01	**-0.40**	-0.11	-0.10	0.25
Diabetes PYLL per 100 000 pop. aged, years 2005–2009 [d]	0.07	0.16	0.12	-0.09	-0.02
Ischaemic heart disease PYLL per 100 000 pop., years 2005–2009 [d]	-0.27	-0.00	0.07	-0.25	**-0.52**
Cerebrovascular disease PYLL per 100.000 pop., years 2005–2009 [d]	-0.21	0.20	0.17	-0.15	**-0.42**
Bronchitis, asthma and emphysema PYLL per 100 000 pop., years 2005–2009 [d]	-0.23	0.08	0.05	**-0.43**	0.02
Concentration Index (very) bad self-rated health, year 2006 [e]	-0.27	-0.26	**-0.43**	0.05	-0.02
Concentration Index asthma prevalence, year 2006 [e]	0.11	0.32	0.04	0.01	0.06
Concentration Index diabetes prevalence, year 2006 [e]	0.05	0.02	0.11	0.12	-0.01

Notes: The matrix provides the results of the Pearson correlation analysis of study variables. The **bold** Pearson correlation indices are statistically significant (p≤.05). COPD – chronic obstructive pulmonary disease; PYLL – potential years of life lost.

a The analyses included data for all 31 participating European countries.
b The analysis included data for 27 countries, excluding Iceland, Norway, Switzerland and Turkey (lack of data).
c The analysis for asthma and COPD included data for 23 countries (excl. Bulgaria, Cyprus, Estonia, Greece, Lithuania, Luxembourg, Romania and Turkey (lack of data); also excluded for diabetes France, Hungary, Slovakia.
d The analysis for diabetes, ischaemic heart disease and cerebrovascular disease included data for 24 countries; excl. Bulgaria, Cyprus, Latvia, Lithuania, Malta, Romania and Turkey; for bronchitis data from 23 countries, also excl. Switzerland.
e The analysis included data for 27 countries, excl. Iceland, Norway, Switzerland and Turkey.

Source: Kringos et al., 2013c.

- Furthermore, it was found that countries with relatively strong primary care have lower socioeconomic inequalities in self-assessed health.

- Primary care strength, however, was not associated with patient ratings of the quality of primary care. Contrary to other studies, it was found that countries with a stronger primary care structure have higher total health care expenditures. However, countries with more comprehensive primary care have a slower growth in health care expenditures.

With regard to the *structure* of primary care, we can conclude that:

- Concerning health care governance, it appeared that important functions were decentralized and that regulation on continuing medical education was a point of attention. Guidelines for GPs were often developed without their involvement.

- Concerning economic conditions, an east–west divide was visible in expenditures and income of providers. In most countries GPs were self-employed.

- An issue of workforce development was the ageing of providers. Workforce plans or forecasting of human resources was unknown in most countries. Nurses in primary care were much less organized than physicians.

For the *process*-related issues of primary care, it appeared that:

- The process of care was relatively well developed in Denmark, Spain and the United Kingdom, but the process dimensions were much more heterogeneous than the structure dimensions.

- A concern on accessibility was the widespread geographical inequalities. In many countries patients need to pay out of pocket for primary care (especially for prescribed medicines). The likelihood that GPs visit patients at home strongly varies between countries. Outside office hours, access to primary care was usually inferior to access during office hours.

- In many countries, informational continuity was not well developed.

- Countries strongly differed in conditions for coordination, such as patients being registered with a GP of their choice. As solo practice dominates primary care, GP practices were small-scale enterprises in many countries.

- The range of services provided by GPs showed different profiles. In countries with gatekeeping GPs, these were particularly strong as the doctor of first contact. Solo GPs provide more follow-up care than GPs working in larger settings.

Our attempt to *explain the variation* led to the following observations:

- In western Europe relatively weaker primary care systems are more frequent:

    ◊ in traditional SHI (or Bismarckian) systems, like Belgium, France and Germany;

    ◊ where primary care is provided in smaller-scale – mainly solo – practices;

    ◊ where there is emphasis on freedom of choice (both for patients and doctors);

◊ where demand for care is channelled via co-payments.

The following features in the national context are associated with strength of primary care:

* *Former communist* countries show the strongest improvement in primary care strength.

* Countries with *social democrat politics* are more likely to have stronger primary care systems.

* *Wealthier* countries are more likely to have weaker primary care systems.

* *Social values* in a country were related to the strength of primary care; for instance values in favour of family care (children taking care of ill parents) were related to weaker primary care systems.

References

Armingeon K et al. (2010). *Comparative political data set III 1990–2008*. Berne, Institute of Political Science, University of Berne.

Boerma WGW, Van der Zee J, Fleming DM (1997). Service profiles of general practitioners in Europe. *British Journal of General Practice*, 47:481–486.

European Observatory on Health Systems and Policies (accessed in 2011). Health System Profiles (HITs) publications.

Groenewegen PP, Delnoij DMJ (2003). De Nederlandse gezondheidszorg in Europees perspectief [The Dutch health care system in European perspective]. In: Aakster CW, Groothof JW (Eds), *Medische sociologie [Medical Sociology]*. Groningen/Houten, Wolters-Noordhof:155–172.

Kringos DS et al. (2013a). The strength of primary care in Europe: an international comparative study. *British Journal of General Practice*, 63(616):e742–e750(9).

Kringos DS et al. (2013b). Political, cultural and economic foundations of primary care in Europe. *Social Science & Medicine*, 99:9–17.

Kringos DS et al. (2013c). Europe's strong primary care systems are linked to better population health, but also to higher health spending. *Health Affairs*, 32(4):686–694.

Pelone F et al. (2013). How to achieve an optimal organization of primary care services delivery at system level: lessons from Europe. *International Journal for Quality in Health Care*, 25(4):381–393.

Sciortino P (2002). A service profile of Maltese general practitioners. A provider survey of the general practice component of the Maltese health care system. Master's thesis, University of Malta, Guardamangia.

Sidel VW, Sidel R (1977). Primary health care in relation to socio-political structure. *Social Science & Medicine*, 11:415–419.

TNS Opinion & Social (2010). *Special Eurobarometer 340 Science and technology*. Brussels, European Commission.

TNS Opinion & Social & TNS (2007). *Special Eurobarometer 283 Health and long-term care in the European Union*. Brussels, European Commission.

WHO Regional Office for Europe (2011). European Health for All Database (HFA-DB) [offline database]. Copenhagen, WHO Regional Office for Europe.

World Values Survey Association (2009). *World Values Survey 1981–2008 official aggregate v.20090901*. Madrid, ASEP/JDS.

Chapter 5

Overview and future challenges for primary care

Wienke Boerma, Yann Bourgueil, Thomas Cartier, Toralf Hasvold,
Allen Hutchinson, Dionne Kringos, Madelon Kroneman

This final chapter places the results of the previous chapters in a broader perspective by sketching the state of primary care in Europe in relation to current and future challenges, and drawing relevant lessons on the basis of the comparative information in this volume.

The PHAMEU study has added evidence to what was known before from international studies. These studies have provided evidence on benefits of well-developed primary care systems, in terms of better coordination and continuity of care and better opportunities to control costs (Starfield, 1994; Delnoij et al., 2000; Shi et al., 2002; Macinko, Starfield & Shi, 2003). The added value of the PHAMEU approach has been that it has covered a larger number of European countries, which makes the results more robust and relevant for Europe.

This chapter is structured as follows. First, the situation of primary care in Europe will be assessed through an overview of the main findings and the results of the in-depth analyses of the PHAMEU data. The subsequent section contains reflections on the findings, including: how the evidence can be applied; an agenda for primary care innovation; developments in the divide between eastern and western Europe; and reflection on essential primary care features like accessibility, equity, integration and skill-mix. Then there is a section devoted to future primary care monitoring, in particular what lessons can be learned from the PHAMEU project. Finally conclusions will be drawn.

5.1 Primary care in Europe today

Overview

The wealth of data collected in the PHAMEU project has shown the complexity and variation in primary care in Europe. Aspects of the structure of primary care (including policies, regulation, financing and workforce) as well as those of service delivery (including accessibility, continuity of care, care coordination and the breadth of the services provided) have been examined. Based on diverse indicators, an overall scoring of the strength of primary care in each country has been established. Countries with the strongest primary care orientation, in terms of its structure and process, were the United Kingdom, Spain, Denmark, the Netherlands and Slovenia. At the other end of the ranking are Cyprus, Luxembourg, Bulgaria, Malta and Greece with relatively weak primary care systems.

The previous chapters have provided important general criteria on the dimensions that make up the state of primary care. It turned out that governance for primary care was well developed across Europe but that the topics of teamwork and multidisciplinary collaboration were poorly addressed. The level of expenditure for primary care differed considerably between countries, but it is noteworthy that in many countries this specification is not available. A distinguishing aspect of workload is the position of nurses in primary care and the role of medical specialists in the provision of primary care services. A general result is the lower status of GPs compared to medical specialists in terms of level of payment.

Accessibility is an essential feature of primary care. Access to services is threatened in countries where there is a shortage of staff. This occurs more frequently in rural areas than in towns and cities and in some countries inequalities are geographically determined. Primary care out of hours usually means provision "out of general practice", at greater distance and run by other doctors. The preparedness of primary care providers to make home visits differs from country to country and this influences the accessibility of home-bound patients to health services. Although there are generally few financial obstacles to visiting general practice, in many countries patients must pay for prescribed medicines.

A referral system, also referred to as gatekeeping, is an agreed powerful function to promote the coordination of care, but is found only in a minority of countries. Some countries have introduced "gate-like" incentives for GPs or patients to promote coordination. An unfavourable condition for coordination is that primary care is still quite fragmented in most countries: solo practice is still the dominant practice situation; also cooperation with medical specialists can be much improved. Coordination with public health services seems to be hardly developed.

Among the clinical tasks of GPs, those related to disease management are usually best developed. The role of providing first-contact care is more developed in countries with a gatekeeping system than in others. The strongest variation is found concerning the provision of medical procedures and minor surgery. In some countries it seems that the provision of such procedures belongs to the domain of the secondary level rather than to general practice. Among the services provided at the primary care level, systematic prevention still seems to be a poorly developed domain. With the available data very little could be concluded about efficiency and the quality of services provided. Differences in workload obviously reflected differences in the position of GPs, but also pointed to possible great differences in efficiency of practice management. The absence of important outcome data for primary care in many countries may be an indication of the modest priority it has in the context of health care in general.

Analytical results

In-depth analyses of the PHAMEU data have shown that in countries with relatively stronger primary care systems, measured by higher scores on the PHAMEU dimensions, population health outcomes are better, socioeconomic inequalities in self-assessed health are smaller and rates of unnecessary hospitalization are lower. However, overall health expenditures were higher in countries with stronger primary care structures. Further research should clarify whether maintaining strong primary care is costly itself or whether other factors are responsible for higher expenditures. It may be concluded that, for Europe, the evidence has grown that strong primary care is conducive to reaching important health system goals.

Furthermore, a country's primary care orientation is influenced by the policy context in a country, which strongly influences priority setting in health care issues as well. Wealthier countries are more likely to have weaker primary care structures and poorer accessibility of primary care in comparison to less wealthy countries. The former communist countries in central and eastern Europe have used their growth of national income to strengthen access to and continuity of primary care. Furthermore, the political landscape in a country was found to be related to the shape of primary care. Countries governed by a predominantly left-wing government over past decades tended to be stronger regarding the structure of primary care as well as with regard to accessibility and the coordination functions.

The lower accessibility and continuity of primary care in countries with a social insurance-based health care system, in contrast to those with NHS-type systems, could be related to the absence of gatekeeping and the use of co-payments, which were more prevalent in systems based on SHI. This was not true, however, for the former communist countries. The issue of "patient choice of provider" is essential in relation to strong primary care. In gatekeeping systems, patients choose a GP to register with and this GP is responsible for access to specialist care for non-emergency cases. Usually patients can change once or twice a year to another GP. In other health care systems, patients are basically free to "self-refer" to any medical specialist. In these countries primary care tasks are carried out by GPs as well as by medical specialists. Sometimes these doctors are in competition for patients. Consequently, GPs in these countries are generally not in the central position that enables them to coordinate care, as in gatekeeping systems.

Findings pointed to contrasting developments between the countries of central and eastern Europe and those elsewhere in Europe. The former communist societies, and the related health care systems, have developed a sharp reaction to their previous highly centralized systems, with their emphasis on specialist and hospital care and no substantial role for primary care in providing health services.

Last but not least, and probably interwoven with the previous point, health care systems appear to reflect something like the national character. Societal values, such as stressing governmental versus individual responsibilities in welfare issues, appeared to be associated with features of the primary care system in a country.

Changes over time

To identify possible changes over the past decades, two studies from the 1990s are relevant. In a study by Macinko and colleagues, the primary care strength of 14 OECD countries was measured in 1995. Although these results are not fully comparable with the results of this study, as the methodology was different and only a limited number of European countries are members of the OECD, it can be observed that in 2009–2010, the primary care strength of Denmark, Greece, Italy, the Netherlands, Norway, Spain, Sweden and the United Kingdom has remained constant, whereas it has improved in Belgium, Finland, France, Germany, Portugal and Switzerland. Moreover, the comparison suggests that the central and eastern European countries have improved their primary care strength since the early 1990s, when they started to transform health care. Many of these countries have retrained physicians to become GPs and have introduced gatekeeping (Liseckiene et al., 2007).

The European GP Task Profile study from 1993 covered almost the same group of countries and provides a good comparison (Boerma & Fleming, 1998). A relevant indicator to compare from this study is the role of GPs as the first contact for health problems (see Fig. 5.1). It turns out that countries where GPs had the strongest first-contact role in 1993 still rank high in primary care strength (see chapter 4, Fig. 4.1). Interesting changes seem to have taken place among the countries where this role of GPs was extremely poor in 1993, namely the former communist countries.

Fig. 5.1

Involvement of GPs in first-contact care in Europe in 1993; range of involvement 1 (low) – 4 (high)

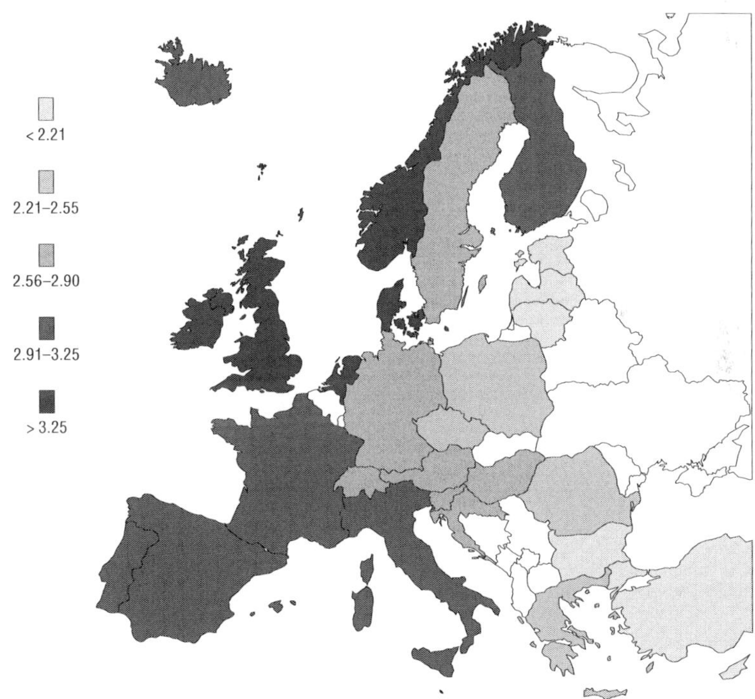

Source: Boerma & Fleming, 1998.

Among these countries, improvements seem to be strong in Lithuania and Estonia, and to some lesser extent also in Romania and Latvia. A strong decline seems to have occurred in Ireland, and Austria has also dropped in this respect. Countries which were at the bottom of the ranking both in 1993 and in 2010 are Bulgaria, Turkey and Greece.

5.2 Implications

Putting the evidence into practice

Although important aspects of effective mechanisms for strong primary care still wait to be understood, it has become increasingly likely that stronger primary care systems are beneficial for health system performance in general, except for expenditures. For policy-makers in Europe who are striving for better-performing health care systems, this is an important message. Putting this evidence into practice requires strategies which may have different accents depending on the health care context and available resources in a country. The study has pointed to various determinants of health care policy, including the economic situation, the national political landscape, the structure of the health care system, and prevailing attitudes and beliefs among the population. However, the results give indications of the issues to address if countries seek to further develop their primary care system.

- The *generic lesson* for policy-makers from the evidence is that strong primary care has an added value for health care in general. However, the evidence also points to *context dependency* when it comes to applying this lesson in a particular country. Indeed, countries can learn from each other how to develop their primary care system, but not by way of copying. What works in one country does not necessarily work in another. For foreign experiences to be applicable in a particular country these need to be "translated" or adapted to be effective and acceptable.

- Through lack of a clear *governmental vision* on the future direction of primary care a framework for action is missing in several countries. A clear central vision is particularly important because most countries have decentralized major primary care functions. Decentralization can increase the responsiveness of primary care at regional or local level, but in the absence of central guidance there is a risk of interregional inequities in access, financing and quality of care.

- *Accessibility and equity,* as core features of any primary care system are at risk as a result of various circumstances. In some countries a shortage of GPs exists in some areas, or a shortage will exist in the near future because the high average age of GPs. Shortages usually arise first in rural areas, thus creating problems of access for the local population. Another problem of access occurs in countries where out-of-hours care is not well organized when primary care practices are closed. Not all people know where to go with health problems outside office hours. They are not always helped adequately. Then, the trend of increasing demand for care of those who are home-bound runs against another trend of GPs making fewer home visits. The growing number of home-bound patients in countries where GPs hardly make home visits may have difficulties with access to medical care. Finally, co-payments can be an obstacle to access and a threat to affordability, in particular to those with low incomes. The highest (formal) payments in the public system exist in Ireland.

- *Integration and coordination* deserve major attention. The lack of multidisciplinary collaboration and teamwork is not only identified as a gap in health policy but also as a weakness in the process of service delivery. The problem is not new, but it is becoming more urgent in the light of growing complexity of care. Breaking down barriers between medical professions and between levels of care could start in medical education and be facilitated by specific incentives. Cooperation and coordination between primary and secondary care might benefit from the creation of multidisciplinary professional education programmes, teamwork and multidisciplinary practices.

- There is an urgent need for countries to take appropriate measures to tackle threatened *workforce shortages*. These could include a regular system of workforce-capacity planning, raising the (financial) attractiveness of the profession, and increasing possibilities for task substitution (OECD, 2010).

- *Patients should be integrated* in health care systems by using their potential for self-management. A challenge related to strong primary care is to create higher satisfaction among patients. In contrast to the positive benefits of strong primary care in terms of cost-containment and health status, results also showed that patients were not more satisfied.

An innovation agenda for the future of primary care

Derived from the challenges that the health sector is currently facing and taking into account what primary care has – potentially – to offer in response to the challenges, a number of specific themes can be identified for primary care in the future, including:

- development of chains of care managed by evidence-based protocols and guidelines, developed by GPs;

- integration of services, between primary and secondary care and with public health;

- integration between the health sector and social services, in particular related to home care (the urgency of this point was recently stressed in a European study on home care (Genet et al., 2012);

- systematic approaches to population-based prevention and health education should be integrated in primary care service routines. This requires better information systems and the application of new technology to support self-monitoring;

- new skill-mixes, in particular new roles for nurses in primary care;

- a new role for patients, shared decision-making and patient empowerment are ingredients to make care for chronically ill people and prevention more effective;

- responsibility for individual episodic patient care should be extended to include the promotion of health and welfare of a community.

Realizing these themes requires various innovations:

- Governance and regulation should encourage cooperation between health care providers; promote the empowerment of patients to better use the relationship with providers; and set targets and facilitate primary care to take up an active role in health promotion and prevention. Legislation and regulation should be developed in the context of an overall vision on the future of primary care and its position within total health care provision.

- Regarding financing, new payment systems, including incentives for integrated care and community orientation, should help new policy aims to be realized.

- In the organization and delivery of service, cooperation and teamwork need to become a high priority. The coordination function of GPs will become increasingly important and larger networks, also referred to as care groups, across levels of care should be developed to better deal with multi-morbidity and chronic conditions. Current obstacles that prevent (chronic) patients flexibly switching between health and social care and between residential care and home care need to be removed.

- The care process should become more patient-centred. Protocols should define patient pathways, including possible needs resulting from multi-morbidity. Individual care plans should facilitate patients to find their way in the complex organization of health care. ICT solutions for more tailor-made care processes should be further developed.

5.3 Primary care in Europe: diversities and similarities

A global view on European primary care systems highlights elements of both similarity and diversity. Despite different historical roots and different reform pathways, there is a considerable degree of coherence among European primary care systems. A major element of similarity is the pre-eminence of GPs as the key focal point of primary care provision, including: being the point of entry to the health care system (though not always the only one); taking a medical advocacy role for individual patients; and acting as the coordinator of the care. These roles are in line with the WONCA Europe definition (Allen et al., 2011). However, not all roles of this definition can be found in all European countries.

The second element of similarity is the formal commitment to universal access to primary care services. This is a distinguishing feature of European primary systems: countries in Europe aim to keep co-payments in primary care low, in particular for visits to GPs. For medicines prescribed in primary care, the situation is different: most countries charge patients for their medicines. Where co-payment for primary care services is required, many countries have established a means for protecting the least advantaged in the population. This issue takes on special importance in the current economic environment where health sector resources are increasingly scarce and co-payments are becoming increasingly prevalent

Elements of diversity: three types

Diversities among European primary care systems are related to the specific cultural and historical backgrounds of each nation, which have had a notable influence on the design of their health care systems. The diversity among the European systems can be captured by a classification in which the following three types of primary care organization are distinguished (Bourgueil, Marek & Mousques, 2009):

- In the *public hierarchical normative model* primary care has a central place in the health care system, and is run by the state rather than by professionals. These systems rely on voluntary coverage mechanisms of the territory by health care facilities, governed by decentralized authorities, for example regions, and which consist of multidisciplinary teams with usually salaried GPs. Examples are Finland, Lithuania, Portugal, Spain and Sweden.

- In the *professional hierarchical gatekeeper model* GPs are the cornerstone and usually in a gatekeeping role. The regulation of accessibility to professionals is less strict than in the previous model. Primary care professionals are also often accountable for the management of resources used for health care. Moreover, the remuneration system of professionals is generally mixed, including capitation mixed with fee for services, in a self-employed position. The pre-eminence of general practice is firmly established through academic excellence in primary care and strong professional associations. Examples are Estonia, Poland, the Netherlands, Denmark, Slovenia and the United Kingdom.

- In the *free professional non-hierarchical model* health professionals try to organize primary care delivery independently, at least without strong regulation from the state or health insurance fund. The model has put emphasis on patients' and professionals' freedom, meaning the absence of a list system or gatekeeping and professionals having a self-employed status. Primary care professionals work alongside each other, in "silos", rather than in a cooperation. Many specialists are also considered as primary care professionals and the academic status of general practice is quite low. Examples are Austria, Belgium, France, Germany and Switzerland.

Not all countries clearly fit into this classification: for example, Italy is at the borders between the first two models, with a decentralization of health care responsibilities, strong willingness to organize primary care at a regional level with advanced primary care management strategies, but with self-employed practitioners paid mainly by capitation, a low academic level for general practice and no nurse practitioners.

The geographical distribution of models is interesting. North-western Europe (Scandinavia, the United Kingdom and the Netherlands) is oriented towards the two first models, whereas western-central Europe, under the historical and cultural influence of France and Germany, is more based on a free professional model (Austria, Belgium and Switzerland, alongside France and Germany). It is also interesting to see how former countries of the eastern bloc chose their primary care policies in the past 20 years, while they were almost all starting from the Soviet Semashko model. There is huge diversity in the choices made.

5.4 Further observations

The vanishing east–west divide

Taking into consideration the history of poorly developed primary care systems in the former eastern bloc countries, the comparison with data from 1993, as was done in chapter 4, highlights an important message (Boerma & Fleming, 1998). The "east–west" contrast that formerly existed in the profile of primary care and the role of primary care providers is currently hardly visible. Nowadays, primary care in Romania, the Czech Republic and Poland is stronger than primary care in Austria. Two Baltic states, Estonia and Lithuania, have even joined the group of stronger primary care systems. In 1993, among the former Soviet bloc countries, the role of GPs as the doctors of first contact was extremely limited, in particular in the Baltic states that were part of the Soviet Union before 1990. An important driver of change in these countries has been the urgent need and the political will to fundamentally break with the past. Besides, however, the accession process to the EU has speeded up the process considerably. Countries with a similar past to the Baltic states, such as Ukraine and Moldova, are currently still far from the level of primary care in the former eastern bloc countries that joined the EU in 2004 (Boerma et al., 2010, 2012).

Keeping the gate

Gatekeeping GPs with registered patients are an important element in strong primary care systems. In countries where they do not exist, however, this seems to be perceived as an unacceptable restriction of the freedom of patients. Countries that do not have a gatekeeping system have tried to introduce gatekeeping elements, usually on a voluntary basis, in order to improve coordination and control the costs of care. Another indication that conditions for coordination and integration are not rapidly improving is the continuing dominance of solo practice in primary care. The question is whether the political will to change this exists. In policy documents interdisciplinary collaboration and integrated care are not major priorities.

New skill-mix

As a consequence of the gradual increase of the package of services provided at the primary care level, including prevention and integrated care for patients with chronic conditions, the current skill-mix deserves to be critically considered. Although new professions enter primary care, such as nurse practitioners, probably more can be expected from an expansion of the current role of nurses. In many countries the nursing potential in primary care is underused. An up-scaling of the tasks of nurses in primary care, which is visible in several countries as an answer to the need for more and complex services, will have consequences for practice management as well.

Primary care research

Information about important performance indicators on quality of care, efficiency, referrals and prescriptions in primary care was not available in many countries. Monitoring without such data is difficult. The poor availability of data may point to a low priority of health services research and, as a consequence, suggest inadequately developed evidence-based policy-making. There is great potential for research into the diversity of health systems in Europe to enable countries to make their systems more efficient and to improve performance. Governments and stakeholders can learn from how other countries deal with shared problems. Although health services research has a high European relevance it is currently not a high priority. The European Commission (EC) budget for health research is mainly devoted to biomedicine, pharmaceuticals and medical technologies (Walshe et al., 2013).

5.5 Options for primary care monitoring

The basis for this book has been a broad implementation of the European Primary Care (PC) Monitor. The question is whether the current structure of the PC Monitor, which is derived from an expert consensus and a literature review of existing concepts in primary care, holds enough information to check if European countries are ready to tackle future issues.

The PC Monitor in the future may be extended to address the challenges identified in the second part of this chapter:

- E-health applications in primary care may be a solution for shortages in remote areas or may help home-bound patients to have contact with their GP, thus substituting for home visits, for example.

- Specialized diagnostic tests directly in primary care practices could be added to the current list of primary care equipment in the indicators for comprehensiveness.

- As migration of the primary care workforce is a growing issue, this could be inserted in the regulatory policies in the governance part of the Monitor; effects of migration on the workforce could be inserted in the workforce development dimension of the Monitor.

- The Monitor should follow the changing service profile in European primary care. A point for consideration will be to include items about services which are currently not frequently offered in primary care or which will be newly developed. More data may be collected on systematic prevention and ways to empower patients for self-care and access to and use of medical information and patients' own medical records.

Information about future challenges that have been identified should lead to new indicators in the context of several dimensions, to cover all their aspects. For instance, for the effects of ageing of the population, information could be gathered on:

- issues concerning the management of ageing, chronic diseases and multi-morbidity by the health care system, both at national and community levels and at policy and delivery levels;

- information on the existence of specific guidelines for primary care management of chronic diseases and multi-morbidity.

Integrated care is becoming an important issue, especially for chronic conditions. Issues addressing financial constructions and cooperation with secondary care could be added.

Balancing the European PC Monitor

A strength of the PC Monitor is that it builds on well-known frameworks for health care system analysis (such as the structure–process–outcome approach) and primary care research. A major building block in its development was carrying out a systematic literature review on primary care. This provided a comprehensive overview of the scientific evidence base for the importance of primary care functions. The results were used for multiple purposes: to identify the key dimensions of primary care, indicators to measure them, and a scoring system for the strength of primary care.

The use of the Monitor also encountered difficulties. Comparing health care systems internationally, for instance, requires taking into account cultural differences between countries. The in-depth analyses have pointed to differences in what is believed to be a good health care system and different values in society as a whole, which may lead to different organization of the health care system. This path dependency makes it difficult to assess and implement good practices.

A limitation mentioned earlier is the availability of data. Although we managed to complete quite a comprehensive primary care data set for all included countries, inevitably not all countries were able to provide data for each indicator. Countries vary much more on data availability on process indicators than on structure indicators. Most countries had very little data available on primary care outcome indicators such as quality and efficiency of care. The identified gaps in available data are likely to reflect a relatively low priority and low level of development of primary care in the respective countries.

The PC Monitor provides a comprehensive, but not exhaustive, overview of the key elements of primary care. By using both quantitative and qualitative indicators, we were able to measure a diverse combination of aspects involved in the structure, organization and performance of primary care. Limited outcome dimensions could be represented, however. Currently, quality and efficiency of care are used, which each have a limited set of indicators, due to a weak evidence base for their suitability as primary care outcome indicators. Also, equity in health is an important health system outcome which could not be represented in the PC Monitor due to a lack of suitable indicators. Nevertheless, aspects that influence equity in use of primary care services are included in the PC Monitor. Commonly applied structure and process indicators of inequalities in primary care access and use have been integrated into several dimensions.

For example, policy on equality in access (governance), primary care coverage (economic conditions), geographic availability of primary care services (access) and affordability of primary care services (access) are all related to equity.

Another strength of the PC Monitor is that it is applicable to different configurations of primary care across Europe. For practical reasons (e.g. availability of data), a sizeable number of indicators (e.g. to measure comprehensiveness of primary care) are still focused on GPs. This is not surprising when considering that GPs are the only professionals that appear as primary care providers in every one of the 31 European countries studied, which facilitates international comparisons. However, this does limit the applicability of certain dimensions of the PC Monitor, given the multitude of other primary care disciplines engaged in the delivery of primary care.

Monitoring for health policy

Evidence-based policy

Policy-makers would be more capable of monitoring the impact of their policies on primary care, and able to evaluate the development of aspects of primary care if they applied a primary care monitoring instrument on a regular basis. The PC Monitor instrument provides a sound tool for monitoring and benchmarking the strength of primary care, and for evaluating primary care in the context of policy aims. By creating a basis for routine data collection, the PC Monitor could serve the need of various stakeholder groups for reliable and comparable information. Application of the Monitor will provide European and national decision-makers with comprehensive comparisons of primary care policies and models of provision.

The OECD has included a small selection of primary care indicators from the PC Monitor in their Second Wave Health System Characteristics Survey. Collecting this data may be a step towards a more regular European information basis for primary care. Such more generic measurement would be a good starting point for countries to benchmark aspects of primary care and select features that require a further in-depth national analysis, for which the PC Monitor indicators can be used.

Data infrastructure

Another point pertains to the improvement of the data infrastructure for primary care. The degree and quality of primary care data availability shows the potential capacity of a country to evaluate and monitor the state of primary care, identify improvement areas, and be accountable and transparent on system performance. In almost all countries high-quality primary care information on comprehensive aspects of the system is lacking. If policy-makers and international health care organizations continue to give primary care a vital role in achieving health system outcomes, there is an urgent need to invest more in improving the primary care information infrastructures, both at national and international level.

International organizations that are currently investing in health system overviews should also focus more on including essential information on primary care in these descriptions. It is justified to invest more in collecting comparable information on the essential features of primary care. For example, it would be valuable if the current Health Systems in Transition publications of the European Observatory on Health Systems and Policies, and the Health Systems and Policy Monitor were to include information on all dimensions of primary care.

5.6 Conclusion

The PHAMEU study has provided a deeper insight into the differences and similarities among national primary care systems in Europe. A major similarity across the countries is the universal coverage of primary care, which is widely achieved, and the position of GPs as the recognized cornerstone of the primary care system. Elements of diversity could be classified according to the relative roles of the medical professions and the state. Irrespective of the model of provision, primary care currently faces challenges resulting from a change of demand from the population, a change of the supply of care, and changes in the financial and technological context. Health care systems will need to adapt to the challenges of multi-morbidity in ageing populations; the expansion of noncommunicable diseases that need to be tackled with new strategies; problems of sustainability and financial constraints and a shrinking workforce. Well-organized and strong primary care may play a major role in successfully coping with these challenges, together with empowered patients. It should be stressed, however, that strategies to develop primary care are necessarily country specific, as the national, social and political context and the history of health care have a strong influence on the organization of care. Although an increasing number of countries have acknowledged the need to further strengthen their primary care systems, information from the PC Monitor has shown the considerable discrepancies between this ideal and the realities in the countries of Europe.

References

Allen J et al. (2011). *The European definition of general practice / family medicine.* WONCA (http://www.woncaeurope.org/content/european-definition-general-practice-family-medicine-edition-2011, accessed March 2014).

Boerma WGW, Fleming DM (1998). *The role of general practice in primary health care.* Copenhagen, The Stationery Office, on behalf of the WHO Regional Office for Europe.

Boerma WGW et al. (2010). *Evaluation of the organization and provision of primary care in Ukraine. A survey-based project.* Copenhagen, WHO Regional Office for Europe.

Boerma WGW et al. (2012). *Evaluation of the organization and provision of primary care in Moldova. A survey-based project.* Copenhagen, WHO Regional Office for Europe.

Bourgueil Y, Marek A, Mousques J (2009). *Three models of primary care organization in Europe, Canada, Australia and New Zealand.* Paris, IRDES (Questions d'économie de la Santé, 141).

Delnoij D et al. (2000). Does general practitioner gatekeeping curb health care expenditure? *Journal of Health Service Research Policy*, 5:22–26.

Genet N et al., eds. (2012). *Home care across Europe: current structure and future challenges.* Copenhagen, WHO Regional Office for Europe.

Liseckiene I et al. (2007). Primary care in a postcommunist country 10 years later: comparison of service profiles of Lithuanian primary care physicians in 1994 and GPs in 2004. *Health Policy*, 83(1):105–113.

Macinko J, Starfield B, Shi L (2003). The contribution of primary care systems to health outcomes within Organisation for Economic Co-operation and Development (OECD), 1970–1998. *Health Service Research*, 38:831–865.

OECD (2010). *International migration of health workers, policy brief.* Paris, Organisation for Economic Co-operation and Development (http://www.oecd.org/dataoecd/8/1/44783473.pdf, accessed February 2014).

Shi L et al. (2002). Primary care, self-rated health, and reductions in social disparities in health. *Health Service Research*, 37:529–550.

Starfield B (1994). Is primary care essential? *The Lancet*, 344:1129–1133.

Walshe K et al. (2013). Health systems and policy research in Europe: Horizon 2020. *The Lancet*, 382:668–669.

Appendix I

The European Primary Care Monitor

Feature	Indicator title	Indicator	Additional information item
GOV1. Primary care goals	Primary care goals	GOV1.1 Have policy documents (by government or important stakeholders) been issued that reflect a clear vision on current and future PC (e.g. for the next five years)? [Yes/No]	GOV1.1a If Yes: In which year? What does this vision entail? What is the status of these documents (e.g. policy paper, law, formal public statement)? Which stakeholder?
GOV2. Policy on equality in access	Policy on distribution of human resources	GOV2.1 Is there an explicit governmental policy to regulate the distribution of PC providers and facilities more evenly? [Yes/No]	GOV2.1a If yes: Please describe the content of these pro-equality measures (e.g. they may be focused on improved working conditions or on obligations for young doctors to work in rural areas).
GOV3. (De) centralization of PC management and service development	PC within the Ministry of Health	GOV3.1 Does PC has its own department or unit within the Ministry of Health? [Yes/No]	GOV3.1a Does PC have a budget that can be distinguished from other sectors, such as specialist care? [Yes/No] If yes, please explain at which level this budget is established (e.g. national, regional).
	PC policy development at regional or local level	GOV3.2 Have responsibilities for PC been decentralized to regional or local level? [Yes/No]	GOV3.2a If yes, please explain which responsibilities have been decentralized to which levels (for instance, setting priorities; aspects of service provision).
	Stakeholder involvement in PC policy development	GOV3.3 Do organizations of stakeholders contribute to PC policy development (e.g. health insurers, medical professionals, or representatives of patients or consumers)? [Yes/No]	GOV3.3a If yes, please explain in which way they contribute to PC policy development (e.g. in regular formal consultations or incidentally and informally).
	(De) centralization of PC service delivery	GOV3.4 Has community influence on the provision of PC services been organized on a national or regional level? [not applicable, it is not used/ yes, on a national level/ yes in some regions/ yes, incidentally at local level]	GOV3.4a If yes, which of the following forms apply: 1. via ownership of PC facilities by authorities: a. state; b. region; c. local 2. (voluntary) patient councils with PC facilities 3. local/ regional/ national PC satisfaction surveys 4. volunteer work in PC facilities 5. other [Please fill in] …
GOV4. PC quality management infrastructure	Coordination of quality management	GOV4.1 If state inspection on health care exists, does it have a specific unit for PC? [Yes/No/Not applicable]	–
	Certification of providers	GOV4.2 Do formal requirements exist for physicians (such as GPs/family doctors) to work in PC? [Yes/No]	GOV4.2a If yes, what are the obligatory professional requirements for physicians to practise in PC? (e.g. having completed postgraduate specialization or obligatory CME). Please specify for GPs/FDs and possible other specialists working in PC.

Feature	Indicator title	Indicator	Additional information item
	Licensing of facilities	GOV4.3 Do formal requirements exist for PC practices or facilities to operate? [Yes/No]	GOV4.3a If yes: What are the requirements for PC practices or facilities to operate?
			GOV4.3b Please mention important voluntary mechanisms to maintain and improve the quality of care (e.g. clinical guidelines, voluntary peer-review mechanisms).
	Development of clinical guidelines	GOV4.4 Have evidence-based clinical guidelines been produced for specific use by GPs? [Yes/No]	GOV4.4a If yes: What is the usual mode of production of these guidelines? 1. Issued by a national agency such as the Ministry of Health [yes/no] 2. Issued by a college or association of GPs [yes/no] 3. Adapted foreign guidelines [yes/no] 4. Developed by medical specialists [yes/no] 5. Other … [fill in]
GOV5. Patient advocacy	Patient rights	GOV5.1 Have any laws/regulations pertaining to the following patients' rights in PC been implemented? 1. Informed consent [Yes/No] 2. Patient access to own medical files [Yes/No] 3. Confidential use of medical records [Yes/No] 4. Availability of a procedure to process patient complaints in PC facilities [Yes/No]	–
GOV6. Multidisciplinary collaboration	Multidisciplinary collaboration	GOV6.1 Has a governmental policy on cooperation or integration of PC services been laid down in a law or policy paper? [Yes/No/Not applicable because no such policy exists]	GOV6.1a If yes, what is the core of this policy and which PC providers are targeted?
ECO1. Primary care expenditure	Total PC expenditure	ECO1.1 Total expenditure on PC as % of total expenditure on health.	–
	Expenditure on prevention and public health	ECO1.2 Total expenditure on prevention and public health as % of total expenditure on health.	–
ECO2. Primary care coverage	Total PC coverage	ECO2.1 % of the population fully covered or insured for PC costs.	–
	GP services coverage	ECO2.2 % of the population covered or insured for costs of GP services (office and at home).	ECO2.2a If co-payment applies, please explain the volume of co-payment.
	Medicines coverage	ECO2.3 % of the population covered or insured for medicines prescribed in primary care/GP.	ECO2.3a If co-payment applies, please explain the volume of co-payment.
	Uninsured population	ECO2.4 % of the population uninsured for medical expenses (this may be an estimation).	–
	Outpatient medical care coverage by social insurance	ECO2.5 Social health insurance coverage for out-patient medical care by % of population.	–
ECO3. Employment status of PC workforce	Employment status of GPs	ECO3.1 % of GPs that are: 1a. Salaried with national, regional or local authorities; 1b. Salaried with other physicians; 2a. Self-employed with contract to health insurance fund(s) or health authority; 2b. Self-employed without contract (paid by patients out of pocket); 3. Other mode.	–

Feature	Indicator title	Indicator	Additional information item
ECO4. Remuneration system of PC workforce	Remuneration system for salaried GPs	ECO4.1 How are salaried GPs paid? 1. Flat salary; 2. Salary related to the number of their patients; 3. Salary related to both the number of their patients and indicators of performance.	ECO4.1a If they receive a performance-related salary: please explain which elements are taken into account.
	Remuneration system for self-employed GPs	ECO4.2 How are self-employed GPs paid? 1. Fee-for-service payment; 2. Capitation payment; 3. Mix of capitation and fee-for-service payment. 4. Mix of capitation and fee-for-service and other specific components (e.g. bonus for working in disadvantaged areas etc.).	ECO4.2a If they receive a payment consisting of components other than capitation or fee-for-service, please explain to what targets or situations these are related.
ECO5. Income of PC workforce	Income of GPs	ECO5.1 What is the (estimated) gross annual income (in euros) of a 'mid-career' GP (about 10 years' experience and with an average size of practice)?	ECO5.1a Does this income include costs for running the practice (premises; equipment; care; employed staff)?
WFD1. Profile of PC workforce	Type of PC professionals	WFD1.1 To which of the following medical, paramedical and nursing disciplines do people have direct access (which means without referral or intervention by another medical provider)? Please indicate on the list and add disciplines if applicable. Also indicate with each discipline whether they exclusively work in PC or also provide services on referral (for instance in another setting, such as a hospital): – GP/Family physician – Gynaecologist/obstetrician – Paediatrician – Specialist of Internal medicine – Ophthalmologist – ENT specialist – Cardiologist – Neurologist – Surgeon – Primary care/GP practice nurse – Specialized nurse (e.g. on diabetes) – Home care nurse – Physiotherapists (ambulatory) – Midwife (ambulatory) – Occupational therapist – Speech therapist – Dentist – Other, namely …	–
	Age distribution GPs	WFD1.2 Average age of practising GPs.	WFD1.2a What is the age distribution among practising GPs? Please fill in the % of GPs who are: <35 years of age; 35–45 years of age; 45–55 years of age; 55+ years of age.
	Workload GPs	WFD1.3 Average number of working hours per week of GPs (including: hours for keeping up to date and for administration; excluding: hours on call during evenings, weekends etc.).	–
WFD2. Status and responsibilities of PC disciplines	Recognition/ responsibilities of GPs	WFD2.1 Have tasks/duties of GPs or family doctors been described in a law or policy document? [Yes/No]	WFD2.1a If yes, please fill in the name of the document, who issued it, and year of issue.

Feature	Indicator title	Indicator	Additional information item
	Financial status of GPs compared to a specialist	WFD2.2 How does the gross annual income (in euros) of a mid-career GP (about 10 years' experience with average size of practice) relate to the gross annual income of the following medical, paramedical and nursing disciplines of the same age? Please give an estimation whether a GP's income is: – Gynaecologist/obstetrician – Paediatrician – Specialist of Internal medicine – Ophthalmologist – ENT specialist – Cardiologist – Neurologist – Surgeon – Primary care/GP practice nurse – Specialized nurse (e.g. on diabetes) – Home care nurse – Physiotherapists (ambulatory) – Midwife (ambulatory) – Occupational therapist – Speech therapist – Dentist	[Much lower/ lower/ equal/ higher/ much higher]
	Attractiveness of FM among medical students	WFD2.3 What % of all medical graduates choose to enrol in postgraduate training in family medicine (within one year of graduation)? (Use the most recent available year, and fill this in) [...%, with reference year ...]	–
WFD3. PC workforce supply and planning	Development of workforce supply	WFD3.1 Please indicate the % by which the supply (total number) of directly accessible medical, paramedical and nursing disciplines has increased [+...%] or reduced [–...%] over the most recent available five-year period. Please also indicate the years applied [Years ...–...]: – GP/Family physician – Gynaecologist/obstetrician – Paediatrician – Specialist of Internal medicine – Ophthalmologist – ENT specialist – Cardiologist – Neurologist – Surgeon – Primary care/GP practice nurse – Specialized nurse (e.g. on diabetes) – Home care nurse – Physiotherapists (ambulatory) – Midwife (ambulatory) – Occupational therapist – Speech therapist – Dentist – Other, namely ...	–
	GP–specialist ratio	WFD3.2 Total number of active GPs as a ratio to total number of active specialists.	–
	Workforce planning	WFD3.3 Are data available from studies on PC workforce capacity needs and development in the future? [Yes/No]	WFD3.3a If yes, for which PC disciplines and what was the latest date of publication?

Feature	Indicator title	Indicator	Additional information item
WFD4. Academic status of PC	Academic status of FM/ general practice	WFD4.1 % of medical universities (or universities with a medical faculty) with a postgraduate programme in family medicine.	WFD4.1a In what year was postgraduate training in family medicine first introduced?
			WFD4.1b How many departments of family medicine are there at medical universities (or universities with medical faculties) in this country?
	FM/ general practice education	WFD4.2 Is family medicine a subject in the undergraduate medical curriculum? [Yes/No]	WFD4.2a What is the duration of a postgraduate programme in family medicine in this country, and how many months do trainees spend in a PC setting?
	Education of nurses in PC	WFD4.3 Is there professional training specifically for: – district or community nurses? [Yes/No] – PC/GP practice nurses? [Yes/No]	WFD4.3a If yes, what is its duration?
WFD5. Medical associations	Professional association of GPs	WFD5.1 Do national associations or colleges of GPs exist in this country? [Yes/No]	WFD5.1a If yes, please provide the name(s), number of GPs who are members, and indicate which of the following activities the association/ organization undertakes: 1. Defending financial/material interests; 2. Professional development (e.g. guideline development); 3. Education; 4. Scientific activities.
	Professional journal on GP	WFD5.2 Is a journal on family medicine/ general practice being published in this country? [Yes/No]	WFD5.2a Please provide its name, number of issues per year, and the number of subscriptions. Also indicate for each journal a characterization of its content [primarily; about 50/50; minor importance]: news; opinions; popular articles; scientific articles (peer reviewed; with abstract in English).
	Professional association of PC nurses	WFD5.3 Do national associations or organizations of PC nurses exist in this country? [Yes/No]	WFD5.3a If yes, please provide the name(s), number of nurses who are members, and indicate which of the following activities the association/ organization undertakes: 1. Defending financial/material interests; 2. Professional development (e.g. guideline development); 3. Education; 4. Scientific activities.
	Professional journal on PC nursing	WFD5.4 Is a professional journal on PC nursing being published in this country? [Yes/No]	WFD5.4a Please provide its name, number of issues per year, and the number of subscriptions.

Feature	Indicator title	Indicator	Additional information item
ACC1. National availability of PC services	Density available PC workforce	ACC1.1 Please provide the total number of directly accessible medical, paramedical and nursing disciplines available per 100 000 population: – GP/Family physician: … – Gynaecologist/obstetrician: … – Paediatrician: … – Specialist of Internal medicine: … – Ophthalmologist: … – ENT specialist: … – Cardiologist: … – Surgeon: … – Neurologist: … – Primary care/GP practice nurse: … – Specialized nurse (e.g. on diabetes): … – Home care nurse: … – Physiotherapists (ambulatory): … – Midwife (ambulatory): … – Occupational therapist: … – Speech therapist: … – Dentist: … – Other, namely: …	
ACC2. Geographic availability of PC services	Availability of GPs by region	ACC2.1 Difference between region, province or state with highest and with lowest density of GPs (per 100 000 population).	ACC2.1a Availability of GPs by region, province or state per 100 000 population.
	Urban–rural availability of GPs	ACC2.2 Difference between average urban density of GPs (per 100 000 population) and average rural density of GPs.	–
	Shortage of GPs	ACC2.3 Do (regional or national) shortages exist of GPs according to usual national norms?	[No shortage/ Shortage in some regions/ Modest shortage nationwide/ Severe shortage nationwide/ Not applicable, because no norms exist]
	Shortage of community pharmacists	ACC2.4 Do problems exist in the availability of medicines in rural areas due to lack of pharmacies? [Yes/No]	–
ACC3. Accommodation of accessibility	Opening hours	ACC3.1 Are GP practices or PC centres obliged to have a minimum number of opening hours or days?	ACC3.1a If yes, how many hours or days?
	Home visits	ACC3.2 Average number of home visits per week per GP.	–
	Organizational access arrangements	ACC3.3 To what extent do the following organizational arrangements commonly exist in GP practices or PC centres? [(almost) always present/ usually present/ occasionally present/ seldom or never present]: 1. Telephone consultations; 2. E-mail consultations; 3. Practices having a web site; 4. Offering special sessions or clinics for certain patient groups (e.g. diabetics, pregnant women, hypertensive patients etc.) 5. Appointment systems for the majority of the patient contacts.	–

Feature	Indicator title	Indicator	Additional information item
	After-hours PC	ACC3.4 To what extent are the following models for the provision of after-hours PC commonly used? [(almost) always used/ usually used/ occasionally used/ seldom or never used]: 1. Practice-based services: GPs within one practice or organized in a group of practices look after their patients on out-of-hours schedules; 2. PC cooperatives: GPs in a region from several groups, supported by additional personnel, provide after-hours PC mostly in non-profit, large-scale organizations, which include telephone triage and advice, office for face-to-face contact, and house calls. 3. Deputizing services (outsourcing): companies employing doctors take over the provision of after-hours care; 4. Hospital emergency departments provide PC by taking care of health problems after office hours; 5. After-hours PC centres: these are (walk-in) centres for face-to-face contact with a GP or nurse; 6. Other out-of-hours PC/GP service schemes in place.	ACC3.4a Please explain if this scheme has been implemented uniformly all over the country or do significant regional differences exist? If "other schemes" are in place, briefly explain services and providers.
ACC4. Affordability of PC services	Cost-sharing for GP care	ACC4.1 Do patients normally need to pay for [no payment/ some payment/ payment of the full amount]: 1. A visit to their GP; 2. Medicines or injections prescribed by their GP; 3. A visit to a specialist prescribed by their GP; 4. A visit of their GP at the patient's home.	ACC4.1a Please explain if exemptions exist for certain groups of patients (which groups; for which services).
	Patient dissatisfaction with PC prices	ACC4.2 % of patients who rate GP care as not very or not at all affordable.	–
ACC5. Acceptability of PC services	Patient satisfaction with access to PC in general	ACC5.1 % of patients who find it easy to reach and gain access to GPs.	–
CON1. Longitudinal continuity of care	Patient list system	CON1.1 Do GPs have a patient list system? [Yes/No]	CON1.1a Average population size per GP.
	Stability of patient–provider relationship	CON1.2 % of patients reporting they visit their usual PC provider for their common health problems.	–
CON2. Informational continuity of care	Medical record keeping	CON2.1 % of GPs keeping (or reporting keeping) clinical records for all patient contacts routinely.	–

Feature	Indicator title	Indicator	Additional information item
	Electronic clinical support systems	CON2.2 To what extent do GPs have a computer at their disposal in their office? [(almost) always/ usually/ occasionally/ seldom or never]	CON2.2a For which of the following purposes do GPs usually use a computer in their practice?: [answer options per category: yes/no] 1. Booking appointments with patients; 2. Writing bills/financial administration; 3. Prescription of medicines; 4. Keeping medical records of patients; 5. Searching for expert information on the internet; 6. Communicating patient information to specialists; 7. Communicating prescriptions to pharmacists.
			CON2.2b Are clinical record systems in PC/GP able to generate lists of patients by diagnosis or health risk? (e.g. patients with asthma or diabetes, or smokers)
	Referral system	CON2.3 To what extent do GPs use referral letters (including relevant information on diagnostics and treatment performed) when they refer to a medical specialist? [(almost) always/ usually/ occasionally/ seldom or never]	–
	Incoming clinical information procedures	CON2.4 Do PC practices receive information within 24 hours about contacts that patients have with out-of-hours services? [(almost) always/ usually/ occasionally/ seldom or never]	–
	Specialist–GP communication	CON2.5 To what extent do specialists communicate back to a referring GP after an episode of treatment? [(almost) always/ usually/ occasionally/ seldom or never]	–
CON3. Relational continuity of care	Physician choice	CON3.1 Are patients free to choose the PC centre and GP they want to register with? [Yes, patients can freely choose any centre or GP/ Patients are free to choose a centre, but they are assigned to a GP in that centre/ Patients are assigned to a centre in their area, but they are free to register with any GP in that centre/ No, patients are assigned to a PC centre in their area, and they are assigned to a GP in that centre]	CON3.1a Please explain if in reality the situation is not as it is intended to be (except for the usual limited choice in rural areas).
	Patient satisfaction	CON3.2 % of patients who are satisfied with: – their relation with their GP/PC physician – with the available time during consultations with their GP/PC physician – their trust in their GP/PC physician – the explanation their GP or PC physician gives of problems, procedures and treatments	–

Feature	Indicator title	Indicator	Additional information item
COO1. Gatekeeping system	Gatekeeping system	COO1.1 Do patients need a referral to access the following medical, paramedical and nursing disciplines? [1. Yes, a referral is normally required; 2. No they have direct access; 3. Direct access is possible if costs of the visit are paid privately (out of pocket or refunded from a complementary insurance)]: – Gynaecologist/obstetrician – Paediatrician – Specialist of Internal medicine – Ophthalmologist – ENT specialist – Cardiologist – Neurologist – Surgeon – Primary care/GP practice nurse – Specialized nurse (e.g. on diabetes) – Home care nurse – Physiotherapists (ambulatory) – Midwife (ambulatory) – Occupational therapist – Speech therapist – Dentist	
COO2. Skill-mix of PC providers	Shared practice	COO2.1 % of PC practices that are: – Single-handed (solo); – 2 or 3 GPs in the same building without medical specialists; – 4 or more GPs in the same building without medical specialists; – Mixed practice with GPs and medical specialists.	–
	Cooperation within PC	COO2.2 Is it common for GPs to have regular face-to-face meetings (at least once per month) with the following professionals? [Yes, it often occurs/ Yes, it usually occurs/ No, it occasionally occurs/ It seldom or never occurs] Please explain. – Other GP(s) – Practice nurse(s) – Nurse practitioner(s) – Home care nurse(s) – Midwife/birth assistant(s) – PC physiotherapist(s) – Community pharmacist(s) – Social worker(s) – Community mental health workers –	–
	Substitution	COO2.3 How usual are the following modes of care by nurses in PC/GP? [very common/ usual/ rare/ uncommon] 1. Nurse-led diabetes clinics in PC/GP 2. Nurse-led health education (e.g. to stop smoking or for pregnant women)	–

Feature	Indicator title	Indicator	Additional information item
COO3. Collaboration of PC–secondary care	Specialist outreach	COO3.1 How common are the following forms of cooperation between GP/PC and medical specialists? [very common/ usual/ rare/ uncommon] 1. Medical specialists visiting a PC practice to provide specialist care normally provided in hospital (replaced specialist care). 2. Medical specialists visiting a PC practice to provide joint care with a GP (joint consultations). 3. Clinical lessons by a medical specialist for GPs.	COO3.1a How common is it that GPs ask (telephone) advice from the following medical specialists?[very common/ usual/ rare/ uncommon] 1. Paediatricians; 2. Internists; 3. Gynaecologists; 4. Surgeons; 5. Neurologists; 6. Dermatologists; 7. Geriatrists.
COO4. Integration of public health in PC	Epidemiological data set	COO4.1 Are clinical patient records from GP/PC used at regional or local level to identify health needs or priorities for health policy? [routinely (health statistics)/ incidentally/ seldom or never used]	–
	Community health surveys	COO4.2 Are community health surveys conducted to improve the quality and responsiveness of PC? [regularly nationwide/ incidentally nationwide/ regularly at local or regional level/ incidentally at local or regional level]	–
COM1. Medical equipment available	Medical equipment available	COM1.1 How common is it that PC facilities have the following equipment available at the premises: [(almost) always available/ usually available/ occasionally available/ seldom or never available] 1. infant scales; 2. glucose tests; 3. dressings/bandages; 4. otoscope; 5. ECG; 6. urine strips; 7. instruments for stitching wounds; 8. gynaecological speculum; 9. peak flow meter	–
COM2. First contact for common health problems	First-contact care	COM2.1 To what extent do patients with the following health problems visit a GP for first contact care? [(almost) always/ usually/ occasionally/ seldom or never]: – Child with severe cough – Child aged 8 with hearing problem – Woman aged 18 asking for oral contraception – Woman aged 20 for confirmation of pregnancy – Woman aged 35 with irregular menstruation – Woman aged 35 with psychosocial problems – Woman aged 50 with a lump in her breast – Man aged 28 with a first convulsion – Man with suicidal inclinations – Man aged 52 with alcohol addiction problems	COM2.1a Please indicate for each health problem to which other specialty(ies) (other than a GP) these patients may (also) address for first contact? (please list 1 or 2, if applicable): – Child with severe cough – Child aged 8 with hearing problem – Woman aged 18 asking for oral contraception – Woman aged 20 for confirmation of pregnancy – Woman aged 35 with irregular menstruation – Woman aged 35 with psychosocial problems – Woman aged 50 with a lump in her breast – Man aged 28 with a first convulsion – Man with suicidal inclinations – Man aged 52 with alcohol addiction problems

Feature	Indicator title	Indicator	Additional information item
COM3. Treatment and follow-up of diseases	Treatment and follow-up of diseases	COM3.1 To what extent do patients with the following diseases receive treatment/follow-up care from their GP? [(almost) always/ usually/ occasionally/ seldom or never]: – Chronic bronchitis – Peptic ulcer – Congestive heart failure – Pneumonia – Uncomplicated diabetes type II – Rheumatoid arthritis – Mild depression – Cancer (in need of palliative care) – Patients admitted to a nursing home/ convalescent home	COM3.1a Which specialties (besides a GP) are (also) treating in the below – mentioned cases? (please list 1 or 2, if applicable): – Chronic bronchitis – Peptic ulcer – Congestive heart failure – Pneumonia – Uncomplicated diabetes type II – Rheumatoid arthritis – Mild depression – Cancer (in need of palliative care) – Patients admitted to a nursing home/ convalescent home
	GP contacts without referral	COM3.2 % of total patient contacts handled solely by GPs without referrals to other providers.	–
COM4. Medical technical procedures	Medical technical procedures	COM4.1 To what extent do GPs or GP/ PC practice nurses carry out the following activities if one of their patients needs it? [(almost) always/ usually/ occasionally/ seldom or never]: – Wedge resection of ingrown toenail – Removal of sebaceous cyst from hairy scalp – Wound suturing – Excision of warts – Insertion of IUD – Removal of rusty spot from the cornea – Fundoscopy – Joint injection – Strapping an ankle – Setting up an intravenous infusion	COM4.1a Which specialties (besides GPs or GP/PC practice nurses) would (also) provide the procedure? (please list 1 or 2, if applicable): – Wedge resection of ingrown toenail – Removal of sebaceous cyst from hairy scalp – Wound suturing – Excision of warts – Insertion of IUD – Removal of rusty spot from the cornea – Fundoscopy – Joint injection – Strapping an ankle – Setting up an intravenous infusion
COM5. Preventive care	Preventive care	COM5.1 To what extent do GPs carry out the following preventive activities? [(almost) always/ usually/ occasionally/ seldom or never]: – Immunization for tetanus – Allergy vaccinations – Testing for sexually transmitted diseases – Screening for HIV/AIDS – Influenza vaccination for high-risk groups – Cervical cancer screening – Breast cancer screening – Cholesterol level checking	COM5.1a Which specialties (besides GPs) would (also) provide the preventive activity? (please list 1 or 2, if applicable): – Immunization for tetanus – Allergy vaccinations – Testing for sexually transmitted diseases – Screening for HIV/AIDS – Influenza vaccination for high-risk groups – Cervical cancer screening – Breast cancer screening – Cholesterol level checking
COM6. Mother and child & Reproductive health care	Mother and child & Reproductive health care	COM6.1 To what extent do GPs provide the following health services to their patients who need them? [(almost) always/ usually/ occasionally/ seldom or never]: – Family planning/ contraceptive care – Routine antenatal care (in line with national scheme) – Routine paediatric surveillance of children up to 4 years	COM6.1a If not the GP, which other specialty(ies) would provide this health service? (please list 1 or 2, if applicable): – Family planning/ contraceptive care – Routine antenatal care (in line with national scheme) – Routine paediatric surveillance of children up to 4 years

Feature	Indicator title	Indicator	Additional information item
		COM6.2 To what extent are GPs (or practice nurses) involved in infant vaccination on: [(almost) always/ usually/ occasionally/ seldom or never]: – diphtheria – tetanus – pertussis – measles – hepatitis B – mumps – rubella	COM6.2a If not the GP or practice nurse, which other specialty(ies) would provide this health service? (please list 1 or 2, if applicable): – diphtheria – tetanus – pertussis – measles – hepatitis B – mumps – rubella
COM7. Health promotion	Health promotion	COM7.1 To what extent do GPs provide the following individual counselling if this is needed in the practice population? [(almost) always/ usually/ occasionally/ seldom or never]: – Counselling in case of obesity – Counselling in case of poor physical activity – Counselling in case of smoking cessation – Counselling in case of problematic alcohol consumption	COM7.1a If not the GP, which other specialty(ies) would provide this counselling? (please list 1 or 2, if applicable): – Counselling in case of obesity – Counselling in case of poor physical activity – Counselling in case of smoking cessation – Counselling in case of problematic alcohol consumption
	Health education (groupwise)	COM7.2 To what extent are GPs (alone or with others) involved in groupwise health education of their patients (on topics like healthy diet; physical activity; smoking; use of alcohol, etc.)? [usual task of GPs/ incidental task/ rarely or never provided by GPs]	COM7.2a If not the GP, which other specialty(ies) would provide this groupwise health education? (please list 1 or 2, if applicable)
QUA1. Prescribing behaviour of PC providers	Annual prescriptions	QUA1.1 The average number of prescriptions annually provided by GPs per 1000 contacts and/or per 1000 registered patients. (Please use latest available data, and indicate the year.)	–
	Antibiotics consumption	QUA1.2 The defined daily doses of antibiotics use in ambulatory care per 1000 inhabitants per day	–
QUA2. Quality of diagnosis and treatment in PC	Avoidable hospitalization	QUA2.1 The number of hospital admissions for people with the following conditions per 100 000 population per year. Please use the latest available data, and indicate the year. – diagnosis of dehydration/ gastroenteritis (ICD-10 codes: E86, K52.2, K52.8, K52.9) – diagnosis of kidney infection (ICD-10 codes: N10, N11, N12, N13.6) – diagnosis of perforated ulcer (ICD-10 codes: K25.0–K25.2, K25.4–K25.6, K26.0–K26.2, K26.4–K26.6, K27.0–K27.2, K27.4–K27.6, K280–282, K284–K286) – diagnosis of pelvic inflammatory disease (ICD-10 codes: N70, N73, N74) – a diagnosis of ear, nose and throat (ENT) infections (ICD-10 codes: H66, H67, J02, J03, J06, J31.2)	–

Feature	Indicator title	Indicator	Additional information item
QUA3. Quality chronic diseases management	Diabetes care	QUA3.1 Crude percentage of the diabetic population aged >25 with cholesterol 5>mmol/ll. (Crude percentage; use latest available year; please indicate the year.)	–
		QUA3.2 Crude percentage of diabetic population aged >25 years with blood pressure above 140/90 mm Hg measured in the last 12 months. (Crude percentage; use latest available year; please indicate the year.)	–
		QUA3.3 Crude percentage of diabetic population aged >25 years with HbA1C > 7.0%. (Crude percentage; use latest available year; please indicate the year.)	–
		QUA3.4 Crude percentage of diabetic population aged >25 years with overweight and obesity and BMI measured in the last 12 months. (Crude percentage; use latest available year; please indicate the year.)	–
		QUA3.5 Crude percentage of diabetic population aged >25 years with eye fundus inspection in the last 12 months. (Crude percentage; use latest available year; please indicate the year.)	–
	COPD care	QUA3.6 Percentage of individuals with COPD who have had a lung function measurement during the last year. (Use latest available year; please indicate the year.)	–
		QUA3.7 Percentage of individuals with COPD that have had a follow-up visit in primary care during the last year. (Use latest available year; please indicate the year.)	–
	Asthma care	QUA3.8 Percentage of individuals with wheeze in the last 12 months or diagnosed with asthma who have had a lung function measurement during the last year. (Use latest available year; please indicate the year.)	–
		QUA3.9 Proportion of individuals having had wheeze in the last 12 months with a diagnosis of asthma who have had a follow-up visit in primary care during the last year. (Use latest available year; please indicate the year.)	–
		QUA3.10 The number of hospital admissions for people with a diagnosis of asthma per 100 000 population per year. (Use latest available year; please indicate the year.)	–
QUA4. Quality of maternal and child health care	Infant vaccination	QUA4.1 % of infants vaccinated within PC against: [% or not applicable because outside PC]: – diphtheria – tetanus – pertussis – measles – hepatitis B – mumps – rubella	–

Feature	Indicator title	Indicator	Additional information item
QUA5. Quality of preventive care	Vaccine preventable ambulatory care sensitive condition	QUA5.1 % population aged 60+ vaccinated against flu. [% or not applicable because outside PC]	–
	Breast cancer screening	QUA5.2 % of women aged 52–69 years who had at least one mammogram in the past three years. [% or not applicable because outside PC]	–
	Cervical cancer screening	QUA5.3 % of women aged 21–64 years who had at least one Pap test in the past three years. [% or not applicable because outside PC]	–
EFF1. General practice efficiency	Home visits	EFF1.1 Number of home visits as % of all GP–patient contacts. (Use latest available year; please indicate the year.)	–
	Telephone consultations	EFF1.2 Number of telephone consultations as % of all GP–patient contacts. (Use latest available year; please indicate the year.)	–
	Duration of GP consultation	EFF1.3 Average consultation length (in minutes) of GPs. (Use latest available year; please indicate the year.)	–
	GP consultations	EFF1.4 Number of GP consultations per capita per year. (Use latest available year; please indicate the year.)	–
	Referrals to medical specialists	EFF1.5 Number of new referrals from GPs to medical specialists per 1000 listed patients per year. (Use latest available year; please indicate the year.)	–

1 Primary care is defined as the first level of professional care where people present their health problems and where the majority of the population's curative and preventive health needs are satisfied.

Appendix II

Scoring of indicators for the European Primary Care Monitor

Dimension: Governance of the PC system

PC system score features and indicators

Component	Indicator	Rationale	Scoring
Primary care goals (GOV1)	**Have policy documents (by government or important stakeholders) been issued that reflect a clear vision on current and future PC (e.g. for the next five years)?** [Yes/No] (GOV1.1)	PC supportive governmental policies are positively associated with adequate access, continuity and coordination of care, the delivery of a wide range of services (in particular preventive care), and better levels of health.[1,2]	1 = No policy documents with clear PC vision 3 = Yes policy documents with clear PC vision are available
Policy on equality in access (GOV2)	**Is there an explicit governmental policy to regulate the distribution of PC providers and facilities more evenly?** [Yes/No] (GOV2.1)	One of the most consistent policy characteristics in countries with a strong PC system is the government's attempts to distribute resources equitably.[1]	1 = No policy on distribution of PC providers 2 = Limited policy on distribution of PC providers available 3 = Yes policy on distribution of PC providers available
(De)centralization of PC management and service development (GOV3)	**Does PC have its own department or unit within the Ministry of Health?** [Yes/No] (GOV3.1)	The creation of a separate PC department within the Ministry of Health improves the role of the government to lead and participate in an effective system of PC governance (e.g. it gives PC a higher priority within the Ministry, can improve relations with other ministries, and provides more systematic, integrated and less fragmented working arrangements).[3]	1 = No PC department at MoH 3 = Yes PC department at MoH
	Does PC have a budget that can be distinguished from other sectors, such as specialist care? [Yes/No] **If yes, please explain at which level this budget is established (e.g. national, regional).** (GOV3.1a)	–	1 = No separate PC budget 3 = Yes separate PC budget
	Have responsibilities for PC been decentralized to regional or local level? [Yes/No] (GOV3.2)	Decentralization of power with the health care decision-making system away from central government to local service delivery creates greater local accountability of services to local populations.[4]	1 = No decentralized PC responsibilities 3 = Yes decentralized PC responsibilities

PC system score features and indicators

Component	Indicator	Rationale	Scoring
	Do organizations of stakeholders contribute to PC policy development (e.g. health insurers, medical professionals, or representatives of patients or consumers)? [Yes/No] (GOV3.3)	To achieve a broad acceptance of PC reforms, it is important to involve stakeholders into the policy process and its implementation, including NGOs and representatives of patients.[3]	1 = No stakeholder involvement in PC policy development 2 = Yes limited stakeholder involvement in PC policy development 3 = Yes stakeholder involvement in PC policy development
	Has community influence on the provision of PC services been organized on a national or regional level? [not applicable, it is not used/ yes, on a national level/ yes in some regions/ yes, incidentally at local level] (GOV3.4)	Community-governed PC practices are more likely to serve the diverse needs of minority populations compared to government-owned PC practices.[5]	1 = No community influence on provision of PC services 2 = Yes community influence on provision of PC services in some regions or incidentally at local level 3 = Yes community influence on provision of PC services on national level or regularly at local level
PC quality management infrastructure (GOV4)	**Does state inspection on health care exist?** [Yes/No] (GOV4.1)	–	1 = No state inspection on health care 3 = Yes there is state inspection in health care
	If state inspection on health care exists, does it have a specific unit for PC? [Yes/No/Not applicable] (GOV4.1a)	The creation of a separate PC department within the Ministry of Health improves the role of the government to lead and participate in an effective system of PC governance.[3]	1 = No PC unit at state Inspection 3 = Yes PC unit at state inspection
	Do formal requirements exist for physicians (such as GPs/family doctors) to work in PC? [Yes/No] (GOV4.2)	(Re)accreditation schemes are a key measure for quality improvement of a health care system. They provide systematic incentives for physicians to keep up certain standards of quality and provide assurance to the public of a physician's basic competence to practise.[6–8]	1 = No PC provider requirements to practise 2 = Yes PC provider requirements to practise exist but exceptions are currently in use 3 = Yes PC provider requirements to practise exist
	Do formal requirements exist for PC practices or facilities to operate? [Yes/No] (GOV4.3)	Specification of requirements for licensing of PC facilities provides assurance to the public of a minimum quality level of PC facilities.[9]	1 = No requirements for PC facilities to operate 3 = Yes requirements for PC facilities to operate
	Have evidence-based clinical guidelines been produced for specific use by GPs? [Yes/No] (GOV4.4)	Developing standards and guidelines to match the needs of general practice is one of the crucial tools in achieving high-quality care.[10] Guidelines are more likely to be appropriately applied when they are the product of one's own profession.[11]	1 = No specific guidelines for GPs 3 = Yes specific guidelines for GPs
Patient advocacy (GOV5)	**Have any laws/regulations pertaining to the following patients' rights in PC been implemented?** **1. Informed consent** [Yes/No] (GOV5.1.1)	Health care legislation is important to protect individuals and communities from harm, and to provide incentives for health care professionals to maintain and/or improve a certain level of service quality.[4]	1 = No informed consent is not regulated 3 = Yes informed consent is regulated

PC system score features and indicators

Component	Indicator	Rationale	Scoring
	Have any laws/regulations pertaining to the following patients' rights in PC been implemented? **2. Patient access to own medical files** [Yes/No] (GOV5.1.2)	Health care legislation is important to protect individuals and communities from harm, and to provide incentives for health care professionals to maintain and/or improve a certain level of service quality.[4]	1 = No patient access to own medical files is not regulated 3 = Yes patient access to own medical files is regulated
	Have any laws/regulations pertaining to the following patients' rights in PC been implemented? **3. Confidential use of medical records** [Yes/No] (GOV5.1.3)	Health care legislation is important to protect individuals and communities from harm, and to provide incentives for health care professionals to maintain and/or improve a certain level of service quality.[4]	1 = No confidential use of medical records is not regulated 3 = Yes confidential use of medical records is regulated
	Have any laws/regulations pertaining to the following patients' rights in PC been implemented? **4. Availability of a procedure to process patient complaints in PC facilities** [Yes/No] (GOV5.1.4)	Health care legislation is important to protect individuals and communities from harm, and to provide incentives for health care professionals to maintain and/or improve a certain level of service quality.[4]	1 = No PC complaint procedures are not regulated 3 = Yes PC complaint procedures are regulated
Multidisciplinary collaboration (GOV6)	**Has a governmental policy on cooperation or integration of PC services been laid down in a law or policy paper?** [Yes/No/Not applicable, because no such policy exists] (GOV6.1)	PC supportive governmental policies are positively associated with adequate access, continuity and coordination of care, the delivery of a wide range of services (in particular preventive care), and better levels of health.[1;2]	1 = No multidisciplinary collaboration policy in place 2 = Limited multidisciplinary collaboration policy in place 3 = Yes a multidisciplinary collaboration policy is in place
Primary care expenditure (ECO1)	**Total expenditure on PC as % of total expenditure on health.** (ECO1.1)	Poor financial investment is one of the impediments to delivery of PC.[12]	1 = <9.80% 2 = 9.80–14.00% 3 = 14.00% > (Percentiles used:33.3% and 66.67% observations)
	Total expenditure on prevention and public health as % of total expenditure on health. (ECO1.2)	Poor financial investment is one of the impediments to delivery of PC.[12]	1 = <2.10% 2 = 2.10–3.50% 3 = 3.50% > (Percentiles used:33.3% and 66.67% observations)
Primary care coverage (ECO2)	**% of the population fully covered or insured for PC costs.** (ECO2.1)	One of the most consistent policy characteristics in countries with a strong PC system is universal financial coverage.[1]	1 = 0–50% covered 2 = 51–74% covered 3 = 75–100% covered (*Little/ no variation*)
	% of the population covered or insured for costs of GP services (office and at home). (ECO2.2) If co-payment applies, please explain the volume of co-payment. (ECO2.2a)	One of the most consistent policy characteristics in countries with a strong PC system is universal financial coverage.[1]	1 = 0–50% covered 2 = 51–74% covered 3 = 75–100% covered (*Little/ no variation*)
	% of the population covered or insured for medicines prescribed in GP/PC. (ECO2.3) If co-payment applies, please explain the volume of co-payment. (ECO2.3a)	One of the most consistent policy characteristics in countries with a strong PC system is universal financial coverage.[1]	1 = 0–50% covered 2 = 51–74% covered 3 = 75–100% covered (*Little/ no variation*)

PC system score features and indicators

Component	Indicator	Rationale	Scoring
	% of the population uninsured for medical expenses (this may be an estimation). (ECO2.4)	One of the most consistent policy characteristics in countries with a strong PC system is universal financial coverage.[1]	1 = 0–50% covered 2 = 51–74% covered 3 = 75–100% covered *(Little/ no variation)*
	Social health insurance coverage for outpatient medical care by % of population. (ECO2.5)	One of the most consistent policy characteristics in countries with a strong PC system is universal financial coverage.[1]	1 = 0–50% covered 2 = 51–74% covered 3 = 75–100% covered *(Little/ no variation)*
Remuneration system of PC workforce (ECO4)	**How are salaried GPs paid? 1. Flat salary; 2. Salary related to the number of their patients; 3. Salary related to both the number of their patients and indicators of performance.** (ECO4.1)	Flexible blended payment methods based on the combination of a fixed component, through either capitation or salary, and a variable component, through FFS, produces a desirable mix of incentives that can change professional behaviour, improve the quality of care and reduce inequalities in the delivery of clinical care. [13–16]	1 = Flat salary 2 = Salary related to patient list 3 = Salary related to patient list and performance indicators
	How are self-employed GPs paid? 1. Fee-for-service payment; 2. Capitation payment; 3. Mix of capitation and fee-for-service payment; 4. Mix of capitation and fee-for-service and other specific components (e.g. bonus for working in disadvantaged areas etc.). (ECO4.2) If they receive a payment consisting of components other than capitation or fee-for-service, please explain to what targets or situations these are related. (ECO4.2a)	Flexible blended payment methods based on the combination of a fixed component, through either capitation or salary, and a variable component, through FFS, produces a desirable mix of incentives that can change professional behaviour, improve the quality of care and reduce inequalities in the delivery of clinical care. [13–16]	1 = FFS or capitation 2 = Mix of capitation and FFS 3 = Mix of capitation and FFS and performance indicators
Income of PC workforce (ECO5)	**What is the (estimated) gross annual income (in euros) of a 'mid-career' GP (about 10 years' experience and with an average size of practice)?** (ECO5.1) Does this income include costs for running the practice (premises; equipment; care; employed staff)? (ECO5.1a)	Poor financial investment and discouraging worker salaries are among the impediments to delivery of PC.[12]	1 = < €37 430.24 2 = €37 430.24–75 789.64 3 = €75 789.64 *(Percentiles used: 33.3% and 66.67% observations)*

PC system score features and indicators

Component	Indicator	Rationale	Scoring
Profile of PC workforce (WFD1)	**To which of the following medical, paramedical and nursing disciplines do people have direct access (which means without referral or intervention by another medical provider)?** (WFD1.1) Also indicate with each discipline whether they exclusively work in PC or also provide services on referral (for instance in another setting, such as a hospital): GP/family physician; Gynaecologist/obstetrician; Paediatrician; Specialist of Internal medicine; Ophthalmologist; ENT specialist; Cardiologist; Neurologist; Surgeon; GP/PC practice nurse; Specialized nurse (e.g. on diabetes); Home care nurse; Physiotherapists (ambulatory); Midwife (ambulatory); Occupational therapist; Speech therapist; Dentist.	Having a medical generalist such as a GP, rather than a specialist as a regular source of care has been associated with better health outcomes and lower health care costs.[1; 17–19] Greater supply of PC providers as opposed to a greater supply of specialty physicians, is consistently associated with better health outcomes.[1; 19] Nursing disciplines and allied health professionals perform services that address health risk behaviours more often than physicians.[20]	1 = PC providers include various medical specialists 2 = PC providers are GPs, OB/GYN and PAED, excluding other medical specialists 3 = PC providers are GPs excluding medical specialists
	Average age of practising GPs. (WFD1.2) What is the age distribution among practising GPs? Please fill in the % of GPs that are: <35 years of age; 35–45 years of age; 45–55 years of age; 55+ years of age. (WFD1.2a)	The key to maintaining a sufficient workforce, in the face of the impending retirement of the "baby boom" generation, is to educate, recruit and retain young practitioners while reinvesting in mature workforce.[21]	1 = Average age of GPs is 55 years > 2 = Majority of GPs are 45–55 years 3 = Average age ≤ 45 years
	Average number of working hours per week of GPs (including: hours for keeping up to date and for administration; excluding: hours on call during evenings, weekends, etc.). (WFD1.3)	When GPs' workload reaches too high a level, this causes a shortage of GP care.[22]	1 = 48.01 hours > 2 = 40.00–48.01 3 = <40.00 hours *(Percentiles used: 33.3% and 66.67% observations)*
Status and responsibilities of PC disciplines (WFD2)	**Have tasks/duties of GPs or family doctors been described in a law or policy document?** [Yes/No] (WFD2.1)	Legal reference to the tasks/duties of GPs/FDs gives formal recognition to the profession as a specific discipline and influences the position it takes in a health care system.[23]	1 = No GP task profile is not formally described 3 = Yes GP task profile is formally described
	How does the gross annual income (in euros) of a mid-career GP (about 10 years' experience with average size of practice) relate to the gross annual income of the following medical, paramedical and nursing disciplines of the same age? (WFD2.2) Please give an estimation whether a GP's income is [much lower/ lower/ equal/ higher/ much higher]: Gynaecologist/obstetrician; Paediatrician; Specialist of Internal medicine; Ophthalmologist; ENT specialist; Cardiologist; Neurologist; Surgeon; GP/PC practice nurse; Specialized nurse (e.g. on diabetes); Home care nurse; Physiotherapist (ambulatory); Midwife (ambulatory); Occupational therapist; Speech therapist; Dentist.	Poor financial investment and discouraging worker salaries are among the impediments to delivery of PC.[12] Comparable levels of remuneration within PC and between PC and secondary care are supportive of a shared care approach which is necessary for the achievement of coordinated care.[24]	1 = (Much) lower compared to the majority of specialists 3 = Equal or higher compared to the majority of specialists

PC system score features and indicators

Component	Indicator	Rationale	Scoring
	What % of all medical graduates choose to enrol in postgraduate training in family medicine? (Use the most recent available year, and fill this in) [...%, with reference year: ...] (WFD2.3)	Greater supply of PC providers, as opposed to a greater supply of specialty physicians, is consistently associated with better health outcomes.[1;19]	1 = <10.0% 2 = 10.0–25.0% 3 = 25.0% > *(Percentiles used: 33.3% and 66.67% observations)*
PC workforce supply and planning (WFD3)	**Please indicate the % by which the supply (total number) of directly accessible medical, paramedical and nursing disciplines has increased [+...%] or reduced [−...%] over the most recent available five-year period.** (WFD3.1) Please also indicate the years applied [Years ...–...]. (WFD3.1): GP/Family physician; Gynaecologist/obstetrician; Paediatrician; Specialist of Internal medicine; Ophthalmologist; ENT specialist; Cardiologist; Neurologist; Surgeon; GP/PC practice nurse; Specialized nurse (e.g. in diabetes); Home care nurse; Physiotherapists (ambulatory); Midwife (ambulatory); Occupational therapist; Speech therapist; Dentist.	Greater supply of PC providers, as opposed to a greater supply of specialty physicians, is consistently associated with better health outcomes.[1;19]	1 = On average, the PC professions have reduced in supply or increased <6.12% 2 = On average, the PC professions have increased in supply 6.12–11.64% 3 = On average, the PC professions have increased in supply 11.64% > *(Percentiles used: 33.3% and 66.67% observations)*
	Total no. of active GPs as a ratio to total no. of active specialists, (WFD3.2)	Greater supply of PC providers, as opposed to a greater supply of specialty physicians, is consistently associated with better health outcomes.[1;19]	1 = <0.25 2 = 0.25–0.50 3 = >0.50 *(Percentiles used: 33.3% and 66.67% observations)*
	Are data available from studies on PC workforce capacity needs and development in the future? [Yes/No] (WFD3.3)	Workforce planning is an important prerequisite for having an efficient and effective workforce.[21]	1 = No workforce data available 3 = Yes workforce data available
Academic status of PC (WFD4)	**% of medical universities (or universities with a medical faculty) with a postgraduate programme in family medicine.** (WFD4.1)	Few opportunities for professional development is one of the impediments to delivery of PC.[12] The establishment of family medicine/general practice university departments and postgraduate training reflect recognition as an academic discipline and as a profession in health care, and contribute to the development of the profession.[7;25]	1 = <66.43% 2 = 66.43–90.00% 3 = 90.00% > *(Percentiles used: 33.3% and 66.67% observations)*
	Is family medicine a subject in the undergraduate medical curriculum? [Yes/No] (WFD4.2)	The development of a PC system starts with setting up a vocational training programme for PC.[25] The availability of skilled and qualified health care providers is a key quality determinant.[21]	1 = No not subject in undergraduate medical curriculum 3 = Yes subject in undergraduate medical curriculum
	Is there professional training specifically for district or community nurses? [Yes/No] (WFD4.3a)	The availability of skilled and qualified health care providers is a key quality determinant.[21]	1 = No professional training for district or community nurses 3 = Yes professional training for district or community nurses

PC system score features and indicators

Component	Indicator	Rationale	Scoring
	Is there professional training specifically for GP/PC practice nurses? [Yes/No] (WFD4.3b)	The availability of skilled and qualified health care providers is a key quality determinant.[21]	1 = No professional training for district or community nurses 3 = Yes professional training for district or community nurses
Medical associations (WFD5)	**Do national associations or colleges of GPs exist in this country?** [Yes/No] (WFD5.1)	The establishment of organized associations or colleges for PC providers is important for the development of the profession and the quality of PC delivery.[11;26]	1 = No national associations or colleges of GPs exist 3 = Yes associations or colleges of GPs exist
	Is a journal on family medicine/ general practice being published in this country? [Yes/No] (WFD5.2)	The existence of a peer-reviewed journal is an important condition for the successful scientific progress of PC.[26]	1 = No journal on family medicine/ general practice is available 3 = Yes a journal on family medicine/ general practice is available
	Do national associations or organizations of PC nurses exist in this country? [Yes/No] (WFD5.3)	The establishment of organized associations or colleges for PC providers is important for the development of the profession and the quality of PC delivery.[11;26]	1 = No national associations or organizations of PC nurses exist 3 = Yes national associations or organizations of PC nurses exist
	Is a professional journal on PC nursing being published in this country? [Yes/No] (WFD5.4) **Please provide its name, number of issues per year, and the number of subscriptions.** (WFD5.4a)	The existence of a peer-reviewed journal is an important condition for the successful scientific progress of PC.[26]	1 = No professional journal on PC nursing is available 3 = Yes a professional journal on PC nursing is available
National availability of PC services (ACC1)	**Please provide the total number of directly accessible medical, paramedical and nursing disciplines available per 100 000 population:** GP/Family physician; Gynaecologist/ obstetrician; Paediatrician; Specialist of Internal medicine; Ophthalmologist; ENT specialist; Cardiologist; Neurologist; Surgeon; GP/PC practice nurse; Specialized nurse (e.g. on diabetes); Home care nurse; Physiotherapists (ambulatory); Midwife (ambulatory); Occupational therapist; Speech therapist; Dentist. (ACC1.1)	Having a medical generalist such as a GP, rather than a specialist as a regular source of care has been associated with better health outcomes and lower health care costs.[1;17–19] Greater supply of PC providers as opposed to a greater supply of specialty physicians, is consistently associated with better health outcomes.[1;19] Nursing disciplines and allied health professionals perform services that address health risk behaviours more often than physicians.[20]	1 = Majority of PC providers are medical specialists (incl. PAED, OB/GYN) 2 = Majority of PC providers are GPs, PAEDs, OB/GYNs and paramedical and nursing disciplines 3 = Majority of PC providers are GPs and paramedical and nursing disciplines
Geographic availability of PC services (ACC2)	**Difference between region, province or state with highest and with lowest density of GPs (per 100 000 population).** (ACC2.1) Availability of GPs by region, province or state per 100 000 population. (ACC2.1a)	Equality in geographical accessibility of PC contributes to an optimal functioning PC system. Geographic areas with a higher PC density than specialist density have lower hospitalization rates for ambulatory care sensitive conditions, better population health, and lower costs.[1;27–29]	1 = >36.47 per 100 000 difference 2 = 17.67–36.47 per 100 000 difference 3 = <17.67 per 100 000 difference *(Percentiles used: 33.3% and 66.67% observations)*

PC system score features and indicators

Component	Indicator	Rationale	Scoring
	Do national norms exist on the (regional or national) supply of GPs? [Yes/No] (ACC2.3a)	The capacity of the PC workforce for a large part determines the accessibility of care, as it reflects the availability of PC services.[31]	1 = No national norms exist on the supply of GPs 3 = Yes national norms exist on the supply of GPs
	Do (regional or national) shortages exist of GPs according to usual national norms? [No shortage/ Shortage in some regions/ Modest shortage nationwide/ Severe shortage nationwide (ACC2.3b)	The capacity of the PC workforce for a large part determines the accessibility of care, as it reflects the availability of PC services.[31]	1 = Severe or modest shortage nationwide 2 = Shortage in some regions 3 = No shortage
	Do problems exist in the availability of medicines in rural areas due to lack of pharmacies? [Yes/No] (ACC2.4)	The capacity of the PC workforce for a large part determines the accessibility of care, as it reflects the availability of PC services.[31]	1 = Yes problems exist in the availability of medicines in rural areas due to lack of pharmacies 3 = No problems exist in the availability of medicines in rural areas due to lack of pharmacies
Accommodation of accessibility (ACC3)	**Are GP practices or PC centres obliged to have a minimum number of opening hours or days?** (ACC3.1)	A minimum number of opening hours or days gives PC a certain predictability for patients as well as physicians.[32]	1 = No minimum opening hours 2 = Yes limited minimum opening hours (advised but not obligatory) 3 = Yes minimum opening hours are obligatory
	Average no. of home visits per week per GP. (ACC3.2)	Efficiency in general practice can be achieved by a decrease in the number of home visits, and by a higher number of telephone contacts.[33]	1 = <2.30 home visits per week per GP 2 = >8.73 home visits per week per GP 3 = 2.30–8.73 home visits per week per GP *(Percentiles used: 33.3% and 66.67% observations)*
	To what extent do *telephone consultations* commonly exist in GP practices or PC centres? [(almost) always present/ usually present/ occasionally present/ seldom or never present] (ACC3.3a)	Timely access to care when it is needed is one of the hallmarks of a high-quality PC system. This can be assured through several organizational arrangements.[31;34–38]	1 = Telephone consultations are seldom or never present 2 = Telephone consultations are occasionally present 3 = Telephone consultations are (almost) always or usually present
	To what extent do *e-mail consultations* commonly exist in GP practices or PC centres? [(almost) always present/ usually present/ occasionally present/ seldom or never present] (ACC3.3b)	Timely access to care when it is needed is one of the hallmarks of a high-quality PC system. This can be assured through several organizational arrangements.[31;34–38]	1 = E-mail consultations are seldom or never present 2 = E-mail consultations are occasionally present 3 = E-mail consultations are (almost) always or usually present
	To what extent do GP practices or PC centres commonly have a *web site*? [(almost) always present/ usually present/ occasionally present/ seldom or never present] (ACC3.3c)	Timely access to care when it is needed is one of the hallmarks of a high-quality PC system. This can be assured through several organizational arrangements.[31;34–38]	1 = PC practice web sites are seldom or never present 2 = PC practice web sites are occasionally present 3 = PC practice web sites are (almost) always or usually present

PC system score features and indicators

Component	Indicator	Rationale	Scoring
	To what extent do GP practices or PC centres commonly *offer special sessions or clinics for certain patient groups* (e.g. diabetics, pregnant women, hypertensive patients, etc.)? [(almost) always present/ usually present/ occasionally present/ seldom or never present] (ACC3.3d)	Timely access to care when it is needed is one of the hallmarks of a high-quality PC system. This can be assured through several organizational arrangements.[31;34-38]	1 = Special sessions or clinics are seldom or never offered 2 = Special sessions or clinics are occasionally offered 3 = Special sessions or clinics are (almost) always or usually offered
	To what extent do GP practices or PC centres commonly use *appointment systems for the majority of patient contacts*? [(almost) always present/ usually present/ occasionally present/ seldom or never present] (ACC3.3e)	Timely access to care when it is needed is one of the hallmarks of a high-quality PC system. This can be assured through several organizational arrangements.[31;34-38]	1 = Appointment systems are seldom or never used 2 = Appointment systems are occasionally used 3 = Appointment systems are (almost) always or usually used
	To what extent are the following models for the provision of after-hours PC commonly used? [(almost) always used/ usually used/ occasionally used/ seldom or never used]: **1. Practice-based services: GPs within one practice or organized in a group of practices look after their patients on out-of-hours schedules; 2. PC cooperatives: GPs in a region from several groups, supported by additional personnel, provide after-hours PC mostly in non-profit, largescale organizations, which include telephone triage and advice, office for face-to-face contact, and house calls. 3. Deputizing services (outsourcing): companies employing doctors take over the provision of afterhours care; 4. Hospital emergency departments provide PC by taking care of health problems after office hours; 5. After-hours PC centres: these are (walk-in) centres for face-to-face contact with a GP or nurse; 6. Other out-of-hours GP/PC service schemes in place.** (ACC3.4)	When PC providers are not accessible for patients at irregular hours, this affects the quality of care appropriate for first-contact health problems. Out-of-hours health care arrangements should therefore be made.[31; 35; 36; 39; 40]	1 = Hospital emergency departments (almost) always or usually provide PC after office hours 2 = After-hours care is occasionally provided within PC 3 = After-hours care is (always or usually) provided within PC
Affordability of PC services (ACC4)	**Do patients normally need to pay for a visit to their GP?** [no payment/ some payment/ payment of the full amount] (ACC4.1a)	One of the most consistent policy characteristics in countries with a strong PC system is low or no patient cost-sharing for PC services.[1]	1 = Payment of the full amount for a visit to their GP 2 = Some payment for a visit to their GP 3 = No payment for a visit to their GP
	Do patients normally need to pay for medicines or injections prescribed by their GP? [no payment/ some payment/ payment of the full amount] (ACC4.1b)	One of the most consistent policy characteristics in countries with a strong PC system is low or no patient cost-sharing for PC services.[1]	1 = Payment of the full amount for medicines or injections prescribed by their GP 2 = Some payment for medicines or injections prescribed by their GP 3 = No payment for medicines or injections prescribed by their GP

PC system score features and indicators

Component	Indicator	Rationale	Scoring
	Do patients normally need to pay for a visit to a specialist prescribed by their GP? [no payment/ some payment/ payment of the full amount] (ACC4.1c)	One of the most consistent policy characteristics in countries with a strong PC system is low or no patient cost-sharing for PC services.[1]	1 = Payment of the full amount for a visit to a specialist prescribed by their GP 2 = Some payment for a visit to a specialist prescribed by their GP 3 = No payment for a visit to a specialist prescribed by their GP
	Do patients normally need to pay for a visit of their GP at the patient's home? [no payment/ some payment/ payment of the full amount] (ACC4.1d)	One of the most consistent policy characteristics in countries with a strong PC system is low or no patient cost-sharing for PC services.[1]	1 = Payment of the full amount for a visit of their GP at the patient's home 2 = Some payment for a visit of their GP at the patient's home 3 = No payment for a visit of their GP at the patient's home
	% of patients who rate GP care as not very or not at all affordable. (ACC4.2)	Financial access to PC services is a key feature of a strong PC system.[1]	1 = 16.0% > of patients who rate GP care as not very or not at all affordable 2 = 6.0–16.0% of patients who rate GP care as not very or not at all affordable 3 = <6.0% of patients who rate GP care as not very or not at all affordable *(Percentiles used: 33.3% and 66.67% observations)*
Acceptability of PC services (ACC5)	**% of patients who find it easy to reach and gain access to GPs.** (ACC5.1)	The acceptability of PC services determines the extent to which the PC service accommodates the patient and the community served, and influences the accessibility of care.[41–43]	1 = <82.7% 2 = 82.7–92.0% 3 = 92.0% > *(Percentiles used: 33.3% and 66.67% observations)*
Longitudinal continuity of care (CON1)	**Do GPs have a patient list system?** [Yes/No] (CON1.1)	Having a defined practice population by means of a patient list system gives incentives for PC providers as well as patients to provide and receive services on a continuous basis. This is beneficial for the provision of PC services in every aspect.[31; 44; 45]	1 = No patient list system 2 = Formal, optional list system 3 = Yes patient list system
	Average population size per GP. (CON1.1a)	Having a defined practice population by means of a patient list system gives incentives for PC providers as well as patients to provide and receive services on a continuous basis. This is beneficial for the provision of PC services in every aspect.[31; 44; 45]	1 = 1774.37 > patients 2 = <1542.66 patients 3 = 1542.66–1774.37 patients *(Percentiles used: 33.3% and 66.67% observations)*
	% of patients reporting to visit their usual PC provider for their common health problems. (CON1.2)	The existence of an ongoing relationship of a patient with a particular provider, rather than with a particular place or no place at all, is beneficial for the quality of care.[1; 46]	1 = <77.8% 2 = 77.8–85.0% 3 = 85.0% > *(Percentiles used: 33.3% and 66.67% observations)*

PC system score features and indicators

Component	Indicator	Rationale	Scoring
Informational continuity of care (CON2)	**% of GPs keeping (or reporting keeping) clinical records for all patient contacts routinely.** (CON2.1)	Systematically keeping medical records is an important measure to achieve informational continuity of care and to facilitate personalized care provision. Both are important for the quality of care.[1;47-49]	1 = < 75% 2 = 75–85% 3 = 85% > *(Little/no variation)*
	To what extent do GPs have a computer at their disposal in their office? [(almost) always/ usually/ occasionally/ seldom or never] (CON2.2) For which of the following purposes are GPs usually using a computer in their practice? [answer options per category: yes/no] 1. Booking appointments with patients; 2. Writing bills/financial administration; 3. Prescription of medicines; 4. Keeping medical records of patients; 5. Searching expert information on the internet; 6. Communicating patient information to specialists; 7. Communicating prescriptions to pharmacists. (CON2.2a) Are clinical record systems in GP/PC able to generate lists of patients by diagnosis or health risk? (e.g. patients with asthma or diabetes, or smokers) [Yes/No] (CON2.2b)	Computerization of practices is becoming increasingly important in PC for the practice of evidence-based medicine, learning and knowledge management, and quality improvement processes. Effective use of computerization applications is beneficial for the efficiency and quality of care.[1; 50-52]	1 = GPs seldom or never (have or) use computers in their office* 2 = GPs occasionally use computers in their office for various purposes* 3 = GPs almost always or usually use computers in their office for various purposes* *Calculate the average score of all items by applying: 1 = 1 for seldom/never comp 2 = 2–4 scores yes 3 = 5–7 scores yes
	To what extent do GPs use referral letters (including relevant information on diagnostics and treatment performed) when they refer to a medical specialist? [(almost) always/ usually/ occasionally/ seldom or never] (CON2.3)	The delivery of cohesive health care depends on the accessibility and exchange of patient information among those involved in the care of a certain patient. The use of referral letters is a necessity to achieve this.[53-56]	1 = GPs seldom or never use referral letters 2 = GPs occasionally use referral letters 3 = GPs almost always or usually use referral letters
	Do PC practices receive information within 24 hours about contacts that patients have with out-of-hours services? [(almost) always/ usually/ occasionally/ seldom or never]. (CON2.4)	To safeguard the quality of care it is important that the regular provider of care receives feedback on patient results of the visits to other care providers, during or after office hours. Besides the necessity for PC providers to stay up to date on the progress of their patients, patients find it easier to obtain information from their regular source of care compared to a specialist.[53; 55; 57]	1 = PC practices seldom or never receive information within 24 hours about contacts that patients have with out-of-hours services 2 = Occasionally 3 = Almost always or usually

PC system score features and indicators

Component	Indicator	Rationale	Scoring
	To what extent do specialists communicate back to a referring GP after an episode of treatment? [(almost) always/ usually/ occasionally/ seldom or never]. (CON2.5)	To safeguard the quality of care it is important that the regular provider of care receives feedback on patient results of the visits to other care providers, during or after office hours. Besides the necessity for PC providers to stay up to date on the progress of their patients, patients find it easier to obtain information from their regular source of care compared to a specialist. [53; 55; 57]	1 = Specialists seldom or never communicate back to referring GP after an episode of treatment 2 = Occasionally 3 = Almost always or usually
Relational continuity of care (CON3)	**Are patients free to choose the PC centre and GP they want to register with?** [Yes, patients can freely choose any centre or GP/ Patients are free to choose a centre, but they are assigned to a GP in that centre/ Patients are assigned to a centre in their area, but they are free to register with any GP in that centre/ No, patients are assigned to a PC centre in their area, and they are assigned to a GP in that centre]. (CON3.1)	A freely chosen PC provider provides better assurance of a good relationship than does assigning a practitioner. The evidence is strong regarding the benefits of an ongoing relationship with a particular provider rather than with a particular place or no place at all.[1]	1 = No, patients are assigned to a PC centre, and a GP 2 = Patients are free to choose a centre, but assigned to a GP or they are assigned to a centre, but free to choose a GP 3 = Yes, patients can freely choose any centre or GP
	% of patients who are satisfied with their relation with their GP/PC physician. (CON3.2a)	The delivery of high quality of care to a large degree depends on the quality of the personal relationship between patients and their PC provider, which ideally is characterized by a sense of responsibility for the delivery of coordinated and comprehensive care, and a mutual feeling of trust and loyalty. [49; 58-62]	1 = On average < 75% of patients are satisfied with their relationship with their GP/PC provider 2 = On average 75–90% of patients are satisfied with their relationship with their GP/PC provider 3 = On average 90% > of patients are satisfied with their relationship with their GP/PC provider
	% of patients who are satisfied with the available time during consultations with their GP/PC physician. (CON3.2b)	The delivery of high quality of care to a large degree depends on the quality of the personal relationship between patients and their PC provider, which ideally is characterized by a sense of responsibility for the delivery of coordinated and comprehensive care, and a mutual feeling of trust and loyalty. [49; 58-62]	1 = On average < 75% of patients are satisfied with the available time during consultations with their GP/PC physician 2 = On average 75–90% of patients are satisfied with the available time during consultations with their GP/PC physician 3 = On average 90% > of patients are satisfied with the available time during consultations with their GP/PC physician

PC system score features and indicators

Component	Indicator	Rationale	Scoring
	% of patients who are satisfied with the explanation their GP or PC physician gives of problems, procedures and treatments. (CON3.2d)	The delivery of high quality of care to a large degree depends on the quality of the personal relationship between patients and their PC provider, which ideally is characterized by a sense of responsibility for the delivery of coordinated and comprehensive care, and a mutual feeling of trust and loyalty. [49; 58–62]	1 = On average <75% of patients are satisfied with the explanation their GP or PC physician gives of problems, procedures and treatments 2 = On average 75–90% of patients are satisfied with the explanation their GP or PC physician gives of problems, procedures and treatments 3 = On average 90% > of patients are satisfied with the explanation their GP or PC physician gives of problems, procedures and treatments
Gatekeeping system (COO1)	**Do patients need a referral to access the following medical, paramedical and nursing disciplines?** [1. Yes, a referral is normally required; 2. No they have direct access; 3. Direct access is possible if costs of the visit are paid privately (out of pocket or refunded from a complementary insurance)]: Gynaecologist/obstetrician; Paediatrician; Specialist of Internal medicine; Ophthalmologist; ENT specialist; Cardiologist; Neurologist; Surgeon; GP/PC practice nurse; Specialized nurse (e.g. on diabetes); Home care nurse; Physiotherapists (ambulatory); Midwife (ambulatory); Occupational therapist; Speech therapist; Dentist (COO1.1)	Gatekeeping systems have multiple positive effects on health care systems. Most importantly gatekeeping has been associated with cost-containment, increased responsiveness to patients' needs and enhanced quality of care. [1; 63–65]	1 = No gatekeeping system in place (they have direct access to the majority of listed physicians) 2 = No gatekeeping, but there are incentives in place (direct access to the majority of listed physicians is possible if costs of the visit are paid privately) 2.5 = Yes, partially gatekeeping system in place (referral for some specialists needed) 3 = Yes, there is a gatekeeping system (a referral is normally required to the majority of listed physicians)
Skill-mix of PC providers (COO2)	% of PC practices that are: – single-handed (solo); – 2–3 GPs in the same building without medical specialists; – 4 or more GPs in the same building without medical specialists; – mixed practice with GPs and medical specialists. (COO2.1)	Group practices and teams with a greater occupational diversity are independently associated with a higher quality of care. [66; 67] Close involvement of generalist clinicians in specialty care leads to more cost-effective care and better health. [52]	1 = Majority of practices are single-handed 2 = Majority of practices are group practices of GPs 3 = Majority of practices are mixed practices of GPs and specialists
	Is it common for GPs to have regular face-to-face meetings (at least once per month) with the following professionals? [Yes, it often occurs/ Yes, it usually occurs/ No, it occasionally occurs/ It seldom or never occurs]. Please explain: Other GP(s); Practice nurse(s); Nurse practitioner(s); Home care nurse(s); Midwife/birth assistant(s); PC physiotherapist(s); Community pharmacist(s); Social worker(s); Community mental health workers. (COO2.2)	Close collaboration between different PC providers optimizes the treatment of patients, and therefore increases the strength of PC. Regardless of the mode of teamwork that is applied, there should be some form of structural communication among PC providers treating mutual patients. [31; 32; 68; 69]	1 = GPs seldom or never have regular face-to-face meetings with various PC providers* 2 = GPs occasionally have regular face-to-face meetings with various PC providers* 3 = GPs often/usually have regular face-to-face meetings with various PC providers* *Calculate the average score of all professions by applying: 1 = seldom or never 2 = occasionally 3 = often/usually

PC system score features and indicators

Component	Indicator	Rationale	Scoring
	How usual are nurse-led diabetes clinics in GP/PC? [very common/ usual/ rare/ uncommon] (COO2.3a)	Efficiency in general practice can be achieved by delegating more tasks to the practice support staff. [33; 42; 70] Nursing disciplines perform services that address health risk behaviours more often than physicians. [19]	1 = Nurse-led diabetes clinics in GP/PC seldom occur 3 = Nurse-led diabetes clinics in GP/PC are common
	How usual is nurse-led health education (e.g. for stopping smoking or pregnant women) in GP/PC? [very common/ usual/ rare/ uncommon] (COO2.3b)	Efficiency in general practice can be achieved by delegating more tasks to the practice support staff. [33; 42; 70] Nursing disciplines perform services that address health risk behaviours more often than physicians.[19]	1 = Nurse-led health education in GP/PC seldom occurs 3 = Nurse-led health education in GP/PC is common
Collaboration of PC–secondary care (COO3)	**How common are the following forms of cooperation between GP/PC and medical specialists?** [very common/ usual/ rare/ uncommon] 1. Medical specialists visiting a PC practice to provide specialist care normally provided in hospital (replaced specialist care). 2. Medical specialists visiting a PC practice to provide joint care with a GP (joint consultations). 3. Clinical lessons by a medical specialist for GPs. (COO3.1)	Shared care arrangements between primary and secondary care providers stimulate mutual education, promote cooperation across levels, improve guideline-consistent care, reduce the use of inpatient services, and improve appropriate prescribing and medication adherence. They thereby improve health outcomes. [39; 53; 56; 71–76]	1 = GPs/PC providers rarely collaborate with specialists* 2 = Various forms of cooperation between GP/PC and specialists usually exist* 3 = Various forms of cooperation between GP/PC and specialists are very common* [13] *Calculate the average score of the three questions by applying: 1 = rare or uncommon 2 = usual 3 = very common
	How common is it that GPs ask (telephone) advice from the following medical specialists? [very common/ usual/ rare/ uncommon] 1. Paediatricians; 2. Internists; 3. Gynaecologists; 4. Surgeons; 5. Neurologists; 6. Dermatologists; 7. Geriatrists. (COO3.1a)	Shared care arrangements optimize patient care and improve health outcomes. Regardless of the mode of cooperation that is applied, there should be some form of structural communication among PC providers treating mutual patients. [31; 32; 68; 69]	1 = GPs rarely ask (telephone) advice from various specialists* 2 = It is common for GPs to ask (telephone) advice from various specialists* *Calculate the average score of the seven professionals by applying: 1 = rare or uncommon 2 = usual ("very common" does not occur)
Integration of public health in PC (COO4)	**Are clinical patient records from GP/ PC used at regional or local level to identify health needs or priorities for health policy?** [routinely (health statistics)/ incidentally/ seldom or never used] (COO4.1)	The effect of PC on improving equity for health depends on the availability of information about patient needs in the various areas in which PC practices are located.[1] Targeting services around locally defined needs is effective in improving the quality and responsiveness of PC. [42]	1 = Seldom or never used 2 = Incidentally 3 = Routinely (health statistics)

PC system score features and indicators

Component	Indicator	Rationale	Scoring
	Are community health surveys conducted to improve the quality and responsiveness of PC? [regularly nationwide/ incidentally nationwide/ regularly at local or regional level/ incidentally at local or regional level] (COO4.2)	The effect of PC on improving equity on health depends on the availability of information about the patient needs in the various areas in which PC practices are located.[1] Targeting services around locally defined needs is effective in improving the quality and responsiveness of PC.[42]	1 = Incidentally at local or regional level 2 = Regularly at local or regional level 3 = Regularly or incidentally nationwide
Medical equipment available (COM1)	**How common is it that PC facilities have the following equipment available at the premises:** [(almost) always available/ usually available/ occasionally available/ seldom or never available] 1. infant scales; 2. glucose tests; 3. dressings/ bandages; 4. otoscope; 5. ECG; 6. urine strips; 7. instruments for stitching wounds; 8. gynaecological speculum; 9. peak flow meter (COM1.1)	Inadequate equipment and supplies are among the impediments to delivery of PC services.[12]	1 = PC facilities have little equipment available at the premises 2 = PC facilities have a limited set of equipment available 3 = PC facilities usually have a comprehensive set of equipment available *Calculate the average score of the nine items by applying: 1 = seldom or never 2 = occasionally 3 = often/usually
First contact for common health problems (COM2)	**To what extent will patients with the following health problems visit a GP for first-contact care?** [(almost) always/ usually/ occasionally/ seldom or never]: Child with severe cough; Child aged 8 with hearing problem; Woman aged 18 asking for oral contraception; Woman aged 20 for confirmation of pregnancy; Woman aged 35 with irregular menstruation; Woman aged 35 with psychosocial problems; Woman aged 50 with a lump in her breast; Man aged 28 with a first convulsion; Man with suicidal inclinations; Man aged 52 with alcohol addiction problems. (COM2.1)	First-contact care by PC providers is essential to address the wide variety and often very basic needs existing in the community.[32; 53; 58; 77–78]	1 = GPs rarely provide first-contact care for new health problems 2 = GPs occasionally provide first-contact care for new health problems 3 = GPs usually provide first-contact care for new health problems *Calculate the average score of the 10 items by applying: 1 = seldom or never 2 = occasionally 3 = often/usually
Treatment and follow-up of diseases (COM3)	**To what extent will patients with the following diseases receive treatment/ follow-up care from their GP?** [(almost) always/ usually/ occasionally/ seldom or never]: Chronic bronchitis; Peptic ulcer; Congestive heart failure; Pneumonia; Uncomplicated diabetes type II; Rheumatoid arthritis; Mild depression; Cancer (in need of palliative care); Patients admitted to a nursing home/ convalescent home. (COM3.1)	The provision of a wide range of services provided by PC providers is associated with better health outcomes at lower costs.[1; 19]	1 = GPs are rarely involved in the treatment and follow-up of diseases in their practice population 2 = GPs are occasionally involved in the treatment and follow-up of diseases in their practice population 3 = GPs are usually involved in the treatment and follow-up of diseases in their practice population *Calculate the average score of the nine items by applying: 1 = seldom or never 2 = occasionally 3 = often/usually

PC system score features and indicators

Component	Indicator	Rationale	Scoring
	% of total patient contacts handled solely by GPs without referrals to other providers. (COM3.2)	First-contact care by PC providers is essential to address the wide variety and often very basic needs existing in the community. [32; 53; 58; 77–78] Having a medical generalist such as a GP, rather than a specialist as a regular source of care has been associated with better health outcomes and lower health care costs.[1; 17–19]	1 = <80.0% 2 = 80.0–92.50% 3 = 92.50% > *(Percentiles used: 33.3% and 66.67% observations)*
Medical technical procedures (COM4)	**To what extent do GPs or GP/PC practice nurses carry out the following activities if one of their patients would need so?** [(almost) always/ usually/ occasionally/ seldom or never]. Wedge resection of ingrown toenail; Removal of sebaceous cyst from hairy scalp; Wound suturing; Excision of warts; Insertion of IUD; Removal of rusty spot from the cornea; Fundoscopy; Joint injection; Strapping an ankle; Setting up an intravenous infusion. (COM4.1) Which specialties (besides GPs or GP/PC practice nurses) would (also) provide the procedure? (please list 1 or 2, if applicable) (COM4.1a)	The provision of a wide range of services by PC providers is associated with better health outcomes at lower costs.[1; 19]	1 = GPs or GP/PC practice nurses are rarely involved in the provision of medical technical procedures 2 = GPs or GP/PC practice nurses are occasionally involved in the provision of medical technical procedures 3 = GPs or GP/PC practice nurses are usually involved in the provision of medical technical procedures [15] *Calculate the average score of the 10 items by applying: 1 = seldom or never 2 = occasionally 3 = often/usually
Preventive care (COM5)	**To what extent do GPs carry out the following preventive activities?** [(almost) always/ usually/ occasionally/ seldom or never]. Immunization for tetanus; Allergy vaccinations; Testing for sexually transmitted diseases; Screening for HIV/AIDS; Influenza vaccination for high-risk groups; Cervical cancer screening; Breast cancer screening; Cholesterol level checking. (COM5.1) Which specialties (besides GPs) would (also) provide the preventive activity? (please list 1 or 2, if applicable) (COM5.1a)	Preventive health care activities are cost-effective in the PC setting, and result in improved levels of population health.[1;58] In general, the provision of a wide range of services by PC providers is associated with better health outcomes at lower costs.[1; 19]	1 = GPs are rarely involved in the provision of preventive care 2 = GPs are occasionally involved in the provision of preventive care 3 = GPs are usually involved in the provision of preventive care *Calculate the average score of the eight items by applying: 1 = seldom or never 2 = occasionally 3 = often/usually
Mother and child & Reproductive health care (COM6)	**To what extent do GPs provide the following health services to their patients who need them?** [(almost) always/ usually/ occasionally/ seldom or never]. – Family planning/ contraceptive care – Routine antenatal care (in line with national scheme) – Routine paediatric surveillance for children up to 4 years (COM6.1) If not the GP, which other specialty(ies) would provide this health service? (please list 1 or 2, if applicable) (COM6.1a)	Preventive health care activities are cost-effective in the PC setting, and result in improved levels of population health.[1;79] In general, the provision of a wide range of services by PC providers is associated with better health outcomes at lower costs.[1; 19]	1 = GPs are rarely involved in the provision of mother and child and reproductive health care 2 = GPs are occasionally involved in the provision of mother and child and reproductive health care 3 = GPs are usually involved in the provision of mother and child and reproductive health care *Calculate the average score of the three items by applying: 1 = seldom or never 2 = occasionally 3 = often/usually

PC system score features and indicators

Component	Indicator	Rationale	Scoring
	To what extent are GPs (or practice nurses) involved in infant vaccination on: [(almost) always/ usually/ occasionally/ seldom or never]. – diphtheria – tetanus – pertussis – measles – hepatitis B – mumps – rubella (COM6.2)	Preventive health care activities are cost-effective in the PC setting, and result in improved levels of population health.[1;58] In general, the provision of a wide range of services by PC providers is associated with better health outcomes at lower costs.[1;19]	1 = GPs are rarely involved in the provision of infant vaccination 2 = GPs are occasionally involved in the provision of infant vaccination 3 = GPs are usually involved in the provision of infant vaccination *Calculate the average score of the seven items by applying: 1 = seldom or never 2 = occasionally 3 = often/usually
Health promotion (COM7)	**To what extent do GPs provide the following individual counselling if this is needed in the practice population?** [(almost) always/ usually/ occasionally/ seldom or never]. – Counselling in case of obesity – Counselling in case of poor physical activity – Counselling in case of smoking cessation – Counselling in case of problematic alcohol consumption (COM7.1) If not the GP, which other specialty(ies) would provide this counselling? (please list 1 or 2, if applicable) (COM7.1a)	Preventive health care activities are cost-effective in the PC setting, and result in improved levels of population health.[1;79] In general, the provision of a wide range of services by PC providers is associated with better health outcomes at lower costs.[1;19]	1 = GPs are rarely involved in the provision of individual counselling for health promotion 2 = GPs are occasionally involved in the provision of individual counselling for health promotion 3 = GPs are usually involved in the provision of individual counselling for health promotion *Calculate the average score of the four items by applying: 1 = seldom or never 2 = occasionally 3 = often/usually
	To what extent are GPs (alone or with others) involved in groupwise health education to their patients (on topics like healthy diet; physical activity; smoking; use of alcohol, etc.)? [usual task of GPs/ incidental task/ rarely or never provided by GPs] (COM7.2)	Preventive health care activities are cost-effective in the PC setting, and result in improved levels of population health.[1;79] In general, the provision of a wide range of services by PC providers is associated with better health outcomes at lower costs.[1;19]	1 = GPs are rarely involved in the provision of groupwise health education 2 = GPs are incidentally involved in the provision of groupwise health education 3 = GPs are usually involved in the provision of groupwise health education

Abbreviations:
PC – primary care; NGOs – non-governmental organizations; FFS – fee-for-service; GPs – general practitioners;
FD – family doctor; GP/PC – general practice/primary care

Two-level model for the calculation of scores

Based on the indicators per country, nine separate dimension scores were calculated by a two-level hierarchical latent regression model. The dependent variable is the scores for every country on the indicators belonging to that dimension. In the fixed part of the model the dimension average is estimated together with the indicator effects (using deviation indicator coding), to control for differences in the indicator averages. In the random part, at level one, the indicator measurement errors are modelled as separate variance terms for every indicator; this controls for differences in the indicators, standard deviations.

At level two the effect for every country on the dimension is modelled, and this is used to calculate country dimension scores. This approach allows the calculation of valid dimension scores even if countries have missing indicators.

References

1. Starfield B, Shi L, Macinko J (2005). Contribution of primary care to health systems and health. *Milbank Quarterly*, 83:457–502.

2. Starfield B (2006). State of the art in research on equity in health. *Journal of Health Politics, Policy and Law*, 31:11–32.

3. Boerma WGW et al. (2009). *Evaluation of the organizational model of primary care in Belarus. A survey-based project in the regions of Minsk and Vitebsk.* Copenhagen, WHO Regional Office for Europe.

4. Scrivens E (2007). The future of regulation and governance. *Journal of the Royal Society for the Promotion of Health*, 127:72–77.

5. Crampton P (2005). The ownership elephant: ownership and community-governance in primary care. *New Zealand Medical Journal*, 118:U1663.

6. Contencin P, Falcoff H, Doumenc M (2006). Review of performance assessment and improvement in ambulatory medical care. *Health Policy*, 77:64–75.

7. Grol R et al. (1997). Systems for quality improvement in general practice. *European Journal of General Practice*, 3:65–68.

8. Tamblyn R et al. (2002). Association between licensure examination scores and practice in primary care. *JAMA – Journal of the American Medical Association*, 288:3019–3026.

9. Kringos DS, Boerma WGW, Pellny M (2009). Measuring mechanisms for quality assurance in primary care systems in transition: test of a new instrument in Slovenia and Uzbekistan. *Quality in Primary Care*, 17(3):165–177.

10. Grol R (1993). Development of guidelines for general practice care. *British Journal of General Practice*, 43:146–151.

11. Roland M, Marshall M (2004). Measuring the quality of primary medical care. In: Jones R et al., eds. *Oxford textbook of primary medical care: principles and concepts (vol. I)*. Oxford, Oxford University Press:464–469.

12. Nelson BD et al. (2003). Multimodal assessment of the primary healthcare system of Serbia: a model for evaluating post-conflict health systems. *Prehospital and Disaster Medicine*, 18:6–13.

13. Campbell S et al. (2007). Quality of primary care in England with the introduction of pay for performance. *New England Journal of Medicine*, 357:181–90+114.

14. Doran T et al. (2008). Effect of financial incentives on inequalities in the delivery of primary clinical care in England: analysis of clinical activity indicators for the quality and outcomes framework. *The Lancet*, 372:728–736.

15. Pink GH et al. (2006). Pay-for-performance in publicly financed healthcare: some international experience and considerations for Canada. *Healthcare Papers*, 6:8–26.

16. Simoens S, Giuffrida A (2004). The impact of physician payment methods on raising the efficiency of the healthcare system: an international comparison. *Applied Health Economics and Health Policy*, 3:39–46.

17. Franks P, Fiscella K (1998). Primary care physicians and specialists as personal physicians: health care expenditures and mortality experience. *Journal of Family Practice*, 47:105–109.

18. Gerritsma JGM, Smal JA (1982). *Werkwijze van huisarts en internist: een vergelijkend onderzoek met behulp van een interactieve patientensimulatie [Working method of GPs and internists: a comparative study using an interactive patient simulation]*. Utrecht: Wetenschappelijke Uitgeverij Bunge.

19. Lee A (2007). Improving health and building human capital through an effective primary care system. *Journal of Urban Health*, 84:i75–i85.

20. Hung DY (2007). Improving the delivery of preventive care services. *Managed Care Interface*, 20:38–44.

21. European Commission (2008). *Green Paper on the European workforce for health*. European Commission. COM(2008) 725 final, 1–14. Brussels, European Commission.

22. Van den Berg M (2010). *Workload in general practice*. Utrecht, NIVEL.

23. Svab I (2004). General practice east of Eden: an overview of general practice in Eastern Europe. *Croatian Medical Journal*, 45:537–542.

24. Bosch WJHM van den, Freeman G (2004). Coordination and continuity of care. In: Jones R et al., eds. *Oxford textbook of primary medical care: principles and concepts (vol. 1)*. Oxford, Oxford University Press: 267–273.

25. Lember M (1996). Revaluation of general practice/family medicine in the Estonian health care system. *European Journal of General Practice*, 2:72–74.

26. Van der Zee, Kroneman MW, Bolibar B (2003). Conditions for research in general practice: can the Dutch and British experiences be applied to other countries, for example Spain? *European Journal of General Practice*, 9:41–47.

27. Parchman ML, Culler S (1994). Primary care physicians and avoidable hospitalizations. *Journal of Family Practice*, 39:123–128.

28. Starfield B et al. (2005). The effects of specialist supply on populations' health: assessing the evidence. *Health Affairs*, Jan.–June:W5-97–W5-107.

29. Welch WP, Miller M, Welch HG (1993). Geographic variation in expenditure for physicians' services in the United States. *New England Journal of Medicine*, 328:621–627.

30. Ansari Z (2007). The concept and usefulness of ambulatory care sensitive conditions as indicators of quality and access to primary health care. *Australian Journal of Primary Health*, 13:91–110.

31. Campbell J et al. (2004). *The future of access to general practice-based primary medical care. Informing the debate.* London, Royal College of General Practitioners:1–38.

32. Boerma WGW, Fleming DM (1998). *The role of general practice in primary health care.* Norwich: The Stationery Office.

33. Schellevis FG, Westert GP, de Bakker DH (2005). The actual role of general practice in the Dutch health-care system: results of the Second Dutch National Survey of General Practice. *Journal of Public Health* (UnitedKingdom), 13:265–269.

34. Engels Y et al. (2005). Developing a framework of, and quality indicators for, general practice management in Europe. *Family Practice*, 22:215–222.

35. Grol R, Giesen P, van Uden C (2006). After-hours care in the United Kingdom, Denmark, and the Netherlands: new models. *Health Affairs (Millwood)*, 25:1733–1737.

36. Leibowitz R, Day S, Dunt D (2003). A systematic review of the effect of different models of after-hours primary medical care services on clinical outcome, medical workload, and patient and GP satisfaction. *Family Practice*, 20:311–317.

37. Salisbury C (2004). Does advanced access work for patients and practices? *British Journal of General Practice*, 54:330–331.

38. van Uden CJ et al. (2006). Out-of-hours primary care. Implications of organisation on costs. *BMC Family Practice*, 7:29.

39. Gruen RL et al. (2003). Specialist outreach clinics in primary care and rural hospital settings. *Cochrane Database of Systematic Reviews*.

40. Hutchison B et al. (2003). Patient satisfaction and quality of care in walk-in clinics, family practices and emergency departments: the Ontario walk-in clinic study. *Canadian Medical Association Journal*, 168:977–983.

41. Arah OA et al. (2006). A conceptual framework for the OECD Health Care Quality Indicators Project. *International Journal for Quality in Health Care*, 18(Suppl. 1):5–13.

42. Chapman JL et al. (2004). Systematic review of recent innovations in service provision to improve access to primary care. *British Journal of General Practice*, 54:374–381.

43. Green A, Ross D, Mirzoev T. Primary health care and England: the coming of age of Alma Ata? *Health Policy*, 80:11–31.

44. Campbell JL (1996). The reported availability of general practitioners and the influence of practice list size. *British Journal of General Practice*, 46:465–468.

45. Groenewegen PP, Hutten JB, van der Velden K (1992). List size, composition of practice and general practitioners' workload in the Netherlands. *Social Science & Medicine*, 34:263–270.

46. van Servellen G, Fongwa M, Mockus D'Errico E (2006). Continuity of care and quality care outcomes for people experiencing chronic conditions: a literature review. *Nursing & Health Sciences*, 8:185–195.

47. Heyerick J et al. (1994). Het gebruik van medische dossiers [The use of medical records]. *Huisarts Nu*, 23(10):390–394.

48. Metsemakers JFM, Tayar D (2004). The medical record. In: Jones R et al., eds. *Oxford textbook of primary medical care: principles and concepts (vol. I)*. Oxford, Oxford University Press:445–449.

49. Saultz JW (2003). Defining and measuring interpersonal continuity of care. *Annals of Family Medicine*, 1:134–143.

50. Campbell SM, Roland MO, Gormanly B (1996). Evaluation of a computerized appointment system in general practice. *British Journal of General Practice*, 46:477–478.

51. McInnes DK, Saltman DC, Kidd MR (2006). General practitioners' use of computers for prescribing and electronic health records: results from a national survey. *Medical Journal of Australia*, 185:88–91.

52. Stille CJ et al. (2005). Coordinating care across diseases, settings, and clinicians: a key role for the generalist in practice. *Annals of Internal Medicine*, 142:700–708.

53. Shi L, Starfield B, Xu J (2001). Validating the adult primary care assessment tool. *Journal of Family Practice*, 50:161.

54. Fletcher RH et al. (1984). Measuring the continuity and coordination of medical care in a system involving multiple providers. *Medical Care*, 22:403–411.

55. Rigby M et al. (1998). Integrated record keeping as an essential aspect of a primary care led health service. *British Medical Journal*, 317:579–582.

56. Winkens R, Wallace P (2004). Interprofessional communication. In: Jones R et al., eds. *Oxford textbook of primary medical care: principles and concepts (vol. I)*. Oxford, Oxford University Press:283–287.

57. Preston C et al. (1999). Left in limbo: patients' view on care across the primary/secondary interface. *Quality in Health Care*, 8:16–21.

58. Ferrer RL, Hambidge SJ, Maly RC (2005). The essential role of generalists in health care systems. *Annals of Internal Medicine*, 142:691–699.

59. Fleming DM (2000). Continuity of care: a concept revisited. *European Journal of General Practice*, 6:140–150.

60. Flocke SA (1997). Measuring attributes of primary care: development of a new instrument. *Journal of Family Practice*, 45:64–74.

61. Hjortdahl P (2004). Continuity of care. In: Jones R et al., eds. *Oxford textbook of primary medical care: principles and concepts (vol. I)*. Oxford, Oxford University Press:249–252.

62. McWhinney IR (1998). Primary care: core values in a changing world. *British Medical Journal*, 316:1807–1809.

63. Bhat VN (2005). Institutional arrangements and efficiency of health care delivery systems. *European Journal of Health Economics*, 6:215–222.

64. Gross R, Tabenkin H, Brammli-Greenberg S (2000). Who needs a gatekeeper? Patients' views of the role of the primary care physician. *Family Practice*, 17:222–229.

65. Verhaak PFM et al. (2004). Demand and supply for psychological help in general practice in different European countries: access to primary mental health care in six European countries. *European Journal of Public Health*, 14:134–140.

66. Ashworth M, Armstrong D (2006). The relationship between general practice characteristics and quality of care: a national survey of quality indicators used in the UK Quality and Outcomes Framework, 2004–5. *BMC Family Practice*, 7:68.

67. Xyrichis A, Lowton K (2008). What fosters or prevents interprofessional teamworking in primary and community care? A literature review. *International Journal of Nursing Studies*, 45:140–153.

68. Griffin J (1996). *The future of primary care: papers from a symposium held on 13th September 1995*. London: Office of Health Economics.

69. Heideman J et al. (2006). De samenwerking tussen huisartsen en de GGZ is voor verbetering vatbaar [The collaboration between GPs and mental health care can be improved]. *TSG: Tijdschrift voor Gezondheidswetenschappen*, 84:22–28.

70. Halcomb EJ et al. (2005). Nursing in Australian general practice: directions and perspectives. *Australian Health Review*, 29:156–166.

71. Bowling A, Bond M (2001). A national evaluation of specialists' clinics in primary care settings. *British Journal of General Practice*, 51:264–269.

72. Parkerton PH, Smith DG, Straley HL (2004). Primary care practice coordination versus physician continuity. *Family Medicine*, 36:15–21.

73. Roland M (2004). The primary–secondary care interface. In: Jones R et al., eds. *Oxford textbook of primary medical care: principles and concepts (vol. I)*. Oxford, Oxford University Press:273–281.

74. Smith SM, Allwright S, O'Dowd T (2007). Effectiveness of shared care across the interface between primary and specialty care in chronic disease management. *Cochrane Database of Systematic Reviews*, CD004910.

75. Starfield BH et al. (1976). Continuity and coordination in primary care: their achievement and utility. *Medical Care*, 14:625–636.

76. Vierhout WP et al. (1995). Effectiveness of joint consultation sessions of general practitioners and orthopaedic surgeons for locomotor-system disorders. *The Lancet*, 346:990–994.

77. Macinko J, Starfield B, Shi L (2003). The contribution of primary care systems to health outcomes within Organisation for Economic Co-operation and Development (OECD) countries, 1970–1998. *Health Service Research*, 38:831–865.

78. Starfield B (1998). *Primary care: balancing health needs, services, and technology*. New York, Oxford University Press.

79. Sans-Corrales M et al. (2006). Family medicine attributes related to satisfaction, health and costs. *Family Practice*, 23:308–316.

80. Wilson A, Childs S (2003). The relationship between consultation length, process and outcomes in general practice: a systematic review. *British Journal of General Practice*, 52:1012–1020.

81. Ferech M et al. (2006). European Surveillance of Antimicrobial Consumption (ESAC): outpatient antibiotic use in Europe. *Journal of Antimicrobial Chemotherapy*, 58:401–407.

82. Ansari Z (2007). A review of literature on access to primary health care. *Australian Journal of Primary Health*, 13:80–95.